Staging Portfolio Secrets

The Academy of Staging and Redesign

How to Knock Out
the Competition and
Build a Six-Figure Business in
Home Staging
Using Your Own High Powered,
Customized
Professional Portfolio

Barbara Jennings
CSS/CRS

Learn the Secrets of the Pros

Barbara Jennings, Author/Consultant/Mentor

BUS000000 BUSINESS & ECONOMICS / General
HOM017000 HOUSE & HOME / Remodeling & Renovation
HOM0030000 HOUSE & HOME / Decorating

ISBN: 978-0-9618026-8-4

1. Home staging – United States. 2. House selling – United States. 3. Interior redesign – United States. 4. Interior decorating – United States. 5. Real Estate Staging – United States.6. Interior Design – United States. I. Title. II. Title: Staging Portfolio Secrets for Home Staging & Interior Redesign Businesses: How to Knock Out the Competition and Build a Six-Figure Income Using Your Own High Powered, Customized Professional Portfolio

1.1, 1.2, 1.3, 1.4, 1.5, 1.6, 1.7, 1.8, 1.9, 1.10, 1.11, 1.12, 1.13, 1.14, 1.15, 1.16, 1.17, 1.18, 1.19, 1.20, 1.21, 1.22, 1.23, 1.24, 1.25

Table of Contents

Chapter One

Building a Six Figure Home Staging and Redesign Business

Building a business requires that you promote or advertise it in some manner – preferably using more than one tactic and strategy. And while there are many strategies that are common to all business, there are some that are particularly useful in a visual business like home staging or interior redesign. Whereas you start with one person, the goal is to spread the word (seeds) to as many people as possible, knowing that as you plant the seeds and feed and water your plants (prospects), they will take root, grow and multiply into hundreds of clients (blossoms).

That is the premise for this book and I'll teach you one of the most effective ways to maximize your contacts and prospects by creating, developing and using your own powerful portfolio (visual aid).

In a visual business, one must use material which is visually effective. It is expected. And good visuals will gain business and poor visuals will impede business. So it is incumbent upon any consultant who wants to thrive and survive to create the kind of visuals that are powerful, informative and motivating.

This can best be accomplished through the creation of a portfolio. So what is a portfolio?

Portfolio is a French word meaning "a portable case of the form of a large book, for holding loose drawings, prints, papers, etc." (Webster's Dictionary).

For our purposes here in this manual, portfolio will refer to a body of work that shows visually what your business and services are all about. The portfolio will be made of items that can include (but not limited to) the following items: photographs, cover letter, biographical information, contact information, brochures, business card, forms, contracts, testimonials, or anything else that you would consider helpful to a prospect with whom you wish to do business.

I have dealt quite sufficiently in other books I've written on how to start, grow, develop and manage a home staging or interior redesign business (see last chapter under Bonuses). So I'm not going to be covering those basic tactics unless I see them in relation to the purpose of this manual: to teach you how to create a meaningful, purposeful and powerful portfolio that you can use to dramatically build your business.

While I anticipate that you're in the business already and that you have started your business because you love the industry and the creative opportunity, I'm also going to assume you don't want to work for free – that you expect compensation from clients for your efforts on their behalf.

And I'm going to also assume that the higher the compensation is, the better. Right?

So the most basic purpose of the portfolio is for you, the home stager or re-designer, to get someone to hire you based on your background and experience.

Creating a portfolio of your work is one of the most important things you can accomplish as a stager or re-designer. Unfortunately, relatively few consultants create portfolios because they find the process daunting are insecure about the quality of their work, or about how well they compare to their peers professionally. In addition, others possibly squirm at the idea that they will have to review thousands of photographs taken over many years. Yet others do not know how to select photographs for a portfolio. Finally, there are those who believe that a portfolio cannot be created by them, that such an endeavor has to be conducted under the control of another person or needs to take place in the context of a retrospective of the consultant's work.

While these concerns are legitimate, they do not constitute the true essence of a portfolio. Assembling a portfolio is not the daunting and frightening task it is touted to be. Let's start by taking a close look at what a portfolio is, proceed to study why it is important to create portfolios of your work, learn how you can create a portfolio of your own work, and finally, learn how to use your portfolio to build a client base.

Quite naturally, the homeowner (or real estate agent) has other goals. They are seeking a quality individual to possibly hire, hopefully someone who has the right level of educational or work-related experience in the industry and someone who can fill the requirements they have in mind to accomplish their goals.

They are looking for someone they feel will be dependable, work hard, be reliable and trustworthy, work for a fee that is affordable and fair, and most importantly of all, make money for them or save them money and accomplish all this in record time.

Generally speaking, in most cases neither side cares all that much about the goals of the other side. Well, the consultant (if smart) probably cares more about the goals of the client but the client really doesn't care too much (if at all) about the goals of the consultant.

Therefore, the key is to figure out the best "fit" for both sides. Even though this can sometimes be both complex and time consuming, a top notch portfolio can expedite the whole process so that it proceeds smoothly and greatly benefits each side.

Always remember this one thing: The home owner or the real estate agent or broker doesn't really care about your goals or your agenda. They have their own agenda which takes their total focus.

For the most part, there is always someone else they are evaluating, some other goals they want to achieve, or someone else they must report to. They don't want to lose money by hiring the wrong person. They don't want to be blamed for the ineptitude of someone else; they don't want to waste valuable time; and they don't want to be embarrassed in front of their family, friends, colleagues, bosses, wife or husband.

This is why they can and will take an abundance of time to consider your competition. Some of them may be excellent judges of talent and character. Some of them may feel very awkward and hesitant to make a decision of any kind. Some of them will have budgetary problems or be under heavy time pressures.

They may not have any other stager or re-designer to compare you with, or they may have several portfolios they are evaluating and people they are interviewing.

One thing is certain, however. If they are willing to set an appointment for an interview, they are not going to waste their valuable time working through a time-consuming process which would leave them uncertain about you and your ability to produce the results they seek.

So the key is patient preparation on your part.

And even then, sometimes all it takes is just being at the right place at the right time. But that's luck.

This manual is being written to give you an edge in every situation, not relying on luck at all, but relying on presenting your business and your professional talents in such a way to give you an edge no matter what type of competition you have. It is also geared to create opportunities where you will likely have *no* competition at all.

As you begin the process of patiently preparing yourself to "sell your talents, expertise and experience", remember that it takes time and effort. Every home owner or agent has their own procedure. With some you will be asked to meet with the owner, the person who has the ability to make an instant decision. Or you may be asked to meet with an agent or the broker who may pass you on to someone else yet again.

But no matter who you start out with, remember one thing. *Presentation is half the battle.* Just knowing this fact you need to make sure that every detail is polished and professionally developed.

You'll want a top-notch biographical sheet that will speak silently on your behalf. You'll want a pictorial portfolio that demonstrates your ability to make significant, important designer changes in multiple environments. You'll want to sharpen your personal appearance and grooming habits to create just the right ambience and aura for yourself.

If you'll do your homework, you'll increase your chances immensely of being hired.

There is a great deal to do first. Take the time to do it so that when you set out to meet with prospects, you'll gain the most success in the shortest amount of time. Do the work necessary so that you'll land projects that are enjoyable and fulfilling. Do the work so that the projects you land will pay you what you are worth and not land you in a dead end zone with problem after problem, paying you little to nothing for your time and effort.

At first, the task will feel daunting.

Don't be fooled by that feeling.

Be willing to be that rare person who is willing to do the things that most people refuse to do. You see, it is common knowledge that 80% of the work is done by 20% of the people. I personally think it's more like 90% vs 10%. There are many people who are lazy, irresponsible or lacking in integrity. There are many people who start businesses with unrealistic goals and expectations.

Those are the people who want to cut corners and who want something for nothing. They may also be people prone to do illegal things to get ahead.

Don't be one of them. Be the person who is willing to work hard, who is willing to get educated, get trained, ask questions, prepare properly. Be the person who is tireless, relentless in your enthusiasm and zeal. You will not only find yourself sought after by agents and homeowners, once you have completed a project, you will find referrals come easily.

You will be a rare "find" because of your secret weapon, which is your willingness to aggressively and joyfully do what others refuse to do or are afraid to do.

I know someone who worked for a company on salary. He worked tirelessly year after year after year. He arrived early and stayed late. He never complained. He did the equivalent of two jobs. No one complimented him; they didn't even seem to notice. He got no bonuses or extra time off.

If he was looking for accolades, he would have been disappointed. Eventually the company hit hard times. All the other employees were given pink slips. But he never got one. He had made himself so indispensable to the owner, he never was in jeopardy of getting laid off or fired. Eventually the owner wanted to sell the company. While he could have sold the company to anyone, he offered it to his faithful employee first, who wound up buying the company for pennies on the dollar (Purchase Price: $50,000 – True Value $350,000).

The prudent person (whether an employee or an independent consultant) is the one who goes beyond the call of duty. This type of person is very rare. While most people keep their eye on the clock, these rare people keep their eyes on the future.

When the clock reaches quitting time, most people fight to see who can get out the door the fastest. But I'm here to tell you that the client (or prospect) is watching and making mental notes to see who is willing to go the extra mile – or the extra 5 minutes or 50 minutes.

Who showed up on time? Who looked and talked professionally? Who had a great portfolio that also made sense? Who answered questions without hesitation? Who stressed benefits rather than features? Who listened effectively? Who communicated effectively? Who responded quickly and efficiently? Who was not only educational and enlightening, but also enjoyable to be with?

Entrepreneurs who arrive late, cut corners, waste time, give inaccurate information, overstate promises, fail to follow up properly and in a timely manner – these are the ones that go down to failure.

Just because negative points are not communicated back to you, doesn't mean they aren't being noted and counted against you.

If you want to be successful as a consultant, you must understand that projects will mainly go to winners, not losers. If you do not present a winning portfolio, you will most likely be passed over.

Demonstrating your integrity and trustworthiness is essential to your success. Go the extra mile as a way of life. If you do, life will repay you with good things and good business, often when you least expect it.

What a Portfolio Is and Is Not

Let's start by taking a look at what a portfolio really is. A portfolio is, literally, a *porte folio*, in French, meaning a page carrier. A *folio* is a large page roughly the size of a single newspaper page. *Porte* means to carry. A *porte folio*, shortened to portfolio in English, is basically a device designed to carry loose pages. The first goal of the *porte folio* we might say is to hold these pages together in a secure place so they do not get lost or damaged. For artists these pages are works of art on paper – for stagers and redesigners, they are pages of before and after pictures.

Although a folio is a large page there is no implied size for the contents of a portfolio. Similarly there is no implied restriction on the nature of the contents placed in a portfolio. These can be drawings, paintings, architectural sketches, photographs, collages, etc. There is also no implied restriction on the type of container to be used. The device used to hold these works of art together, the *porte* part of the *porte folio*, can be a folder, a box or some other container chosen by the artist. Finally, there are no restrictions on who can create a portfolio. It is most often the artists or consultants themselves who create portfolios of their work.

Portfolios and <u>Portfolios</u>

In today's digital age, and in theory, a portfolio no longer needs to be printed. It can be created solely through digital means, either from scanned or digital photographs color corrected and optimized then presented in PDF, jpeg or other platform-independent (preferably) format.

Doing so is a perfectly legitimate way to present and select images. However, in my view a portfolio is not a portfolio unless it consists of images printed on paper. Why? For the simple reason that in my eyes a final image is an image on paper, not an image on a computer monitor. There is a tremendous difference between looking at an image on screen and looking at an image on paper. For me, the end product of my efforts is a practical, versatile representation of my work. Of course my way is not the only way, so your opinion may differ. However, if you do not print your work you are missing one of the greatest rewards offered by photography: looking at a print which embodies not only your abilities as a photographer but also your abilities as a printer – and giving you and your prospect the easiest method to discuss your work without the need of a computer or some other type of equipment.

Photos in This Book

The photos in this book are printed in black and white due to the huge expense in printing books with color images. Alas, we would love to show them to you in color, but then we'd have to charge a good deal more for this book. Please understand our predicament. The photos are also mostly candid shots taken by us or by other stagers or re-designers in the business and are not done by professional photographers. They are what they are. Our purpose is not to dazzle you with photographic quality but to teach you how to create your own portfolio and use it to garner clients. The photos we include are sometimes very poor quality to illustrate a point or they may demonstrate what not to do.

Then there is the difficulty of printing photos on high speed digital presses (another problem altogether). So we've done our best with the photos under the circumstances and budget allowed to keep costs down for readers and to show you a "real world" glimpse into the types of photos you're bound to be creating and utilizing in your own portfolio.

Goal and Purpose

It is important to consider your goal and your purpose before creating a portfolio. Doing so will make the process a lot easier. Let me use my work as an example.

I photograph for a purpose. Currently this purpose is to show the beauty and the positive aspects of the interior and exterior of a client's home. My purpose is also to create photographs that might used to sell homes.

Audience

You also need to consider the audience to whom you will show your portfolio.

An audience does not necessarily consist of a large group of people. Some of us have small audiences, consisting of only a single person, while some of us have large audiences, consisting of thousands or millions of people visiting a website. However, regardless of the size of your audience, you do have to consider the relationship between your work and your audience.

To help you understand your relationship to your audience ask yourself the following questions:

– Which images do I want to show to my audience?

– Are there images I want to leave out and not show to my audience?

– Does my work address a single audience, or do some of my photographs address one audience while other photographs address a different audience?

– What kind of response do I want from my audience? Do I want to please my audience, surprise them, or challenge them?

Your goal, purpose and audience may or may not be similar to mine. What is important is that you are aware of their existence and of their importance. Deciding on the contents of your portfolio will be a lot easier if you know the answers. Knowing this will allow you to make informed choices in

regards to the photographs you choose and the mission statement you write.

Unlike an artist who may show photos of a wide variety of subjects (as shown here), as a stager or re-designer, your work will probably be restricted to pictures of homes. Though you might also include some close-ups of wall groupings, custom floral arrangements, accessory arrangements, table arrangements and so forth.

15

I want here to propose a much wider use of portfolios:

Portfolios can be used to show the results of specific work and present one's work up to the time a portfolio is created.

Approached that way portfolios are easier to assemble and far less daunting or frightening. It also becomes clear that there can be many uses for a portfolio, each one tailored to different goals, purposes and audiences. I will discuss this at length in this manual.

For example you can create:

A portfolio that includes photographs from a single camera format (35mm, medium format, large format).

A portfolio which includes only black and white or sepia photographs – where all other consultants will do color – would have some dramatic possibilities.

The Contents of a Portfolio

Photographs are only part of the total content of a portfolio. After all, this is your opportunity to express yourself in ways other than with photographs. It is your opportunity to write, to talk about what you do, to explain why and how your projects were managed and what your clients thought of your work. Here is a short list of what you can include in a portfolio:

A consultant's statement and biographical information

A title list of the projects included in the portfolio

A cover image representative of the portfolio as a whole or full page images used as dividers for different sections

Before and after pictures of each home shown, price range, how long on market after staged, selling price

A sheet of testimonials or several letters of reference

Pictures of you with your family, doing hobbies, etc. to help you establish some common ground

Graph paper for their convenience

Samples of contracts and forms

A brochure and your business card

Copy of your certification certificate, awards you've earned (even if not in this industry)

A nice portfolio encasement

A music CD of classical or easy listening music to be listened to while viewing the work

Selecting Photographs to Include

One of the most difficult aspects of creating a portfolio is selecting the photographs you want to include in your portfolio. There are many photos you want to keep for the future, but not necessarily use in your portfolio. I suggest you save all of your photos on CDs, as well as your hard drive. I've suffered the loss of photos myself and they can never be recouped. I also know of many a home stager and re-designer who has neglected to save photos in multiple places only to lose them forever.

To make the final choices: start by selecting the images you really like by going back through your files, either looking at originals on film or at raw files, prints, digital images, etc. Pull out all the ones you like and get them all in one place or one folder, if possible. You may have a combination of prints, transparencies and digital images on screen. At this stage this is not a problem.

Focus on finding the images that best show a dramatic transition from the way the home looked before I started and the way it looked after I finished. I also consider which images are repetitive. I do this by asking myself if my selection contains images that all "say the same thing" so to speak. If yes, I place these images next to each other to isolate them from the others. I then select the strongest one amongst them.

The key here is to be "tough" with yourself. Some of your favorites will make it into the final cut and others will not make it. The goal is to assemble a portfolio that achieves the goal and purpose you defined previously, a portfolio that will address the audience you have in mind. Here is the process I recommend as a starting point:

1 – Decide how many images you want in your portfolio. I recommend a relatively low number, about 12 to 25 images, so that you have to make a rigorous selection. If you decide to include 100 images for example, the number is so high that it will not allow you to make a rigorous selection.

2 – If you use several camera formats, decide if you want to focus on a particular format (35mm, medium format or 4x5 for example). If this is not the case skip this step.

3 – Make your selection progressively. Start by selecting 100 images or so. Then clear your mind, relax, and when you are ready go back to your selection and now reduce it to 50. Do a third round and now limit it to 12 or 20 images only.

Take a break between each selection, at least a day, and go back to your selection, this time pulling out your favorite images from the selection you made before. I know, those are already all favorites. This is where it gets tough. You have to narrow it down to the favorites of the favorites.

4 – Making the final cut is the most difficult part because it means eliminating images that you like very much. If making the final cut from transparencies or digital files is too difficult, choose only small prints (8x10's) from your selection and make the final selection from these prints. Make high quality prints so that you are making a decision based on what your portfolio images will actually look like.

5 – Get feedback from friends, family members and fellow consultants to see if they agree with your selection. Show them both the final selection (if you have completed it) and the "best 50" selection in case you missed something that everyone believes should be in your portfolio

6 – When going through this process keep in mind that as consultants we are not necessarily the best judges of our work. I base this remark on my personal experience. Learning to identify your strongest work is not easy. I therefore recommend that you not only distance yourself from your work as much as possible (I know how difficult that is) but that you also ask other people which are their favorites. If several persons like the same project it is very likely that you have a winner and that you should include it in your portfolio, even if this image isn't at the top of your list. Of course, you are the final judge, and there may be instances in which you want to make a different choice. However, my personal experience has taught me to listen what others say.

Vary Your Portfolio

Consider ways to vary the way your projects will appear to your audience. Select images that show as many different aspects of your project as possible. For example, include photographs taken with different focal lengths. Include close ups and wide angle views, details and wide scenes. In this approach you are not only looking for your best images, you are also looking for images that complement each other, images that work well together when viewed as a set. For this reason, whenever possible it helps when the vantage point (where you're standing) is the same in the before shot as it is in the after shot. Don't forget that a portfolio is a collection of images, and that these images need to stand out on their own as well as fit into the theme of the portfolio.

A trick that photographers often use who shoot homes for real estate agents, is to mark a spot on the floor with a dot (label) or with masking tape when they take their "before" pictures. Then when they return to capture the "after" pictures, they stand in the same place indicated on the floor.

This is fine, so long as these markers don't show up in your pictures from the other side of the room. You don't want to have to touch up your photos if you don't have to. I find that if I shoot from each of the four corners, and from the middle of each wall, it's not difficult to remember to return to those exact spots at the end of the project.

Cover Image

Finally, select one single image as the "title" or cover image. This may be the most difficult part of all, but it is one of the most important aspects of this project. This image needs to stand for what the portfolio represents, for the message you are sharing through your work. It needs to be strong as a single image and be representative of the portfolio as a whole.

What a Portfolio Is Not

I started this chapter referring to the reasons why few consultants create portfolios of any substance. This is because there seems to be a myth floating around:

- The Portfolio can only show the best work a consultant has ever done. Since it is difficult to really know what our best work actually is (because we're naturally biased), many consultants just can't make the appropriate choices.

- Consultant's always fear they don't have enough to put into a portfolio, so they never get around to making one.
- Some consultants think that creating a portfolio is pretentious or intimidating, so they postpone making one until their work "gets better".

Unfortunately, the end result is that they either never make one to show or they only put partial effort into making it a good one. Either way, they shoot themselves in the foot, so to speak.

If you perceive the task as too difficult and do nothing, preferring to put off the "task" for the future rather than face the critiques now, you will not be the only loser. Your future prospects will lose out as well, because you will have failed to help them see the benefits of your services and left them to be victimized by lesser talent in the industry.

Portfolios are not merely a way to display one's best work – but they are the means to display YOUR work and to help other people see the service and how it might help them.

Most people are visual learners. So your visuals, together with your verbal comments, questions and answers, are key to your success and your ability to help your prospects and clients see the vision and derive all the benefits you can give them.

Chapter Two

Discovering Your Accomplishments

Making the perfect connection that lands you the project is easy when you know how. The problem with most stagers and re-designers is they are too eager to land a project (any project), so they concentrate on looking for simple projects that pay very little. The easy projects require low qualifications. I call these "consults".

These are the projects where you agree to show up and give some little bit of advice for a small fee. Some people are so eager to get "hired" for anything, they find themselves going out for free and letting a home owner or agent "pick their brain" for free.

When someone gets something for free, they usually don't value it. They overwork you, eat up your time, pay you nothing and do nothing with the advice you gave them anyway.

You may find that you're being rejected even when you're looking to get just a consultation, without doing the actual hard work. You may be competing for mere consultations and getting passed over in favor of your competition.

If this continues, you will get discouraged and despondent. Given enough time, you will close your business and go look for a job as an employee somewhere.

But if you will apply what you learn in this manual, you will go a long way to helping yourself land all the business you want, plus moving you into a bona fide career level business of your own, doing what you want to do and what you like to do and getting paid what you're worth.

Much of the material here is from my own personal experience as well as the experiences of my students who have gone on to create outstanding businesses in every part of the country and around the globe.

I will be giving you assignments that will cause you to look inward and assess your talents and your background and experience to date. These exercises will concentrate on your accomplishments so far, as well as your past successes. They are designed to help you see how terrific you already are and how much you have to offer to the industry.

Everyone I have ever taught has underestimated their own qualifications for how they present themselves and their services. Many of my students have fallen into a rut of concentrating on qualities they lack. Negative focus only generates fear and self-doubt – so we must concentrate your efforts on the positive.

Many people believe that we learn best from our past mistakes. Nonsense. We learn best from our successes, even if those successes are not in our present field of endeavor. So we will be looking at your past successes before you ever got into home staging or redesign.

Actually, regarding our past mistakes, the truth is this – the best we can do with mistakes is to learn from them, so that we don't make the same mistakes again. Our mistakes are not the best way to learn. It is what we learn from our successful actions that count. Our learning curve was fruitful and the actions taken were appropriate. Our attitude was also good.

This is not to say that we cannot improve on each of these areas to increase our learning curve in a positive manner. We learn best from our successes since our mistakes cannot produce these types of results.

Truth be known, our mistakes can often be so painful and embarrassing we refuse to think about them any more and certainly don't wish to study them closely. We have all made mistakes. But the secret is in not letting them get us down or keep us from moving on. All our mistakes actually teach us is what not to repeat.

I'm inherently a risk-taker. I tend to believe I can do anything I want to do once I know how, so I'm willing to gamble on myself. I have "stubbed my toe" many times, but I refuse to quit growing or taking risks. I needed to know this about myself in order to find a direction that was suitable for me.

But while I have looked at my past mistakes, I do not dwell on them as that would set me up for future failure. And you must not dwell on yours either. What you focus on is what will increase in your life.

Just as it is true that success breeds success, so also failure breeds failure. It's good to admit our mistakes – that proves we have the integrity to recognize the truth and have a willingness to learn and grow.

But never should we concentrate on our mistakes! Instead, let's concentrate on our successes and our accomplishments and those things we have done for which we can be proud. Then let our portfolios develop from that study and research. Then we can go on to build a truly powerful business.

From time to time I have had to fail a consultant on the exam for certification or I've had to "set aside" the designation of a consultant going through certification based on a portfolio submission to us that was not up to our standards.

It's tough to write and tell someone that their work does not meet our standards. I must inform them of the decision, but also impart insight into the things that we see in their pictures that just don't work. It's tough to be critical and yet try to preserve their spirit and urge them to revisit these issues and turn in more examples for us to preview.

The real winners are the consultants that take the critique to heart and go back and look at the work and study the comments we have made to them and come back with much improved work. Some go back to the homes and make the suggested alterations and learn from that experience and submit pictures of the changes they made.

A few are never heard from again, which is sad, because it's a learning experience and not every one passes on the first round in any venture, and certainly not ours. This is why it's alarming that so many people enter the field and go out and start work without really knowing what they are doing and having little to no accountability for their talents and knowledge.

I see my role as a trainer to oversee my certification candidates to make sure they are on solid ground. It's excellent for the student and excellent for the industry. But this also makes my program tougher to achieve, but also makes the designation of my certification so much more powerful, legitimate and beneficial in the end.

What is An Accomplishment?

An accomplishment is a *combination of feelings because of an experience.* It is something you have done which you feel you have done well, and which you enjoyed.

It is important to concentrate on your accomplishments, looking at them only in terms of how you **feel** about them. Never mind what anyone else thinks about what you have done. We're concentrating here on **your** personal feelings. After all, you are searching for what you want to do with your business, so the only opinion that matters is yours. No one else can determine what will make you happy, fulfilled and satisfied. So never give anyone else that kind of power over your life and your business.

The second rule, if you will, is to decide what you want from your business. To be happy in your work, you must decide what you want the business to provide you over future years. One important factor will be to note what you have already done that has given you pleasure and satisfaction. To do this you need to look not only at your past experience but at your whole life. You will find many of your accomplishments and skills have developed over the years in areas which were not project-related areas or former jobs or careers.

As you move through this manual, you will find that your achievements hold the keys to what fulfills you and gives you pleasure. This insight will be compiled into a sensible, concise statement – a biographical sheet – that will be one of the new tools you will use in your portfolio to help you make those great business connections and land those higher paying projects.

In the process, don't deny past mistakes. You have them. So do I. So does everyone. Big deal. You must be willing to risk, make more mistakes, discover why they occurred, make new successes, study those and move on.

Learning From Mistakes

Back in the early 1980s, when times were economically tough, I started a wicker furniture store. Wicker was the home fashion craze of top interior designers and was predicted to be "hot" for another 15 years.

However, almost immediately after opening my store, the country slid into a recession. Unemployment rose and no one was buying furniture – not even wicker. I did not do a proper job of doing my homework. Within a short period of time I closed the doors forever on my wicker venture.

It was a colossal failure but I learned one especially important lesson from it. I learned I could survive making such a terrible mistake. And I've gone on from that mistake to become a wiser decision-maker.

Other lessons I learned: Not to mortgage my home to generate capital for a business venture, particularly one I knew nothing about and had no prior experience in doing. That was a biggie!

I learned that just because I wanted to succeed, that was not enough in and by itself. I learned that I had under capitalized my venture, that I knew next to nothing about selling or advertising. I learned I knew nothing about picking a good location, that I knew nothing about the perils of a lease.

I learned that I knew nothing of real value about how to choose inventory, much less about where to get my inventory for a true wholesale price. I could fill pages about my lack of knowledge and experience, but you get the picture.

Quite frankly, I had no business starting a wicker furniture business, particularly in a difficult economic time and requiring serious capital investment on top of that, which put my home in jeopardy on top of that.

Was I stupid? Duh!

But I believed I could do anything.

Painful. But I learned. I survived and I'm better off now, but I don't recommend it as a way to learn.

What You Want vs. What You Don't Want

There is a big difference between NOT getting what you DON"T want and getting what you DO want. It's just as it is in athletics – teams which, instead of "playing to win" start "playing not to lose". They end up losing – achieving precisely what they were focused on.

I don't want to be a secretary. Not that secretarial work is beneath me (I did it for many, many years). I just don't want to be a secretary any more. I would be a secretary if there was nothing else for me to do, but since there is, I choose to do something I like. And there's a big difference in not getting to be a secretary and in getting to do what I enjoy – helping people like you succeed in home staging and/or interior redesign. It makes me happy to help you get where you want to go.

So your first step is to be in charge of your direction. You decide what to do with your business. No one cares as much about it as you do. And you alone hold the key to your own success.

Assignment No. 1

So here is your first assignment:

Look carefully at your many accomplishments. Take a sheet of paper (or write directly in this manual) and number it from 1-20 down the left side. Briefly list 20 of your most significant achievements. They don't have to be in chronological order nor even in the order of importance. Just begin writing down your achievements as they come to mind.

Don't select achievements others think are your most important. Here your opinion is the only one that counts.

Your achievements need to meet the following criteria:
1) They must be something you feel you did well;
2) They must be something you enjoyed doing; and
3) They must be something you are proud of having accomplished. Put on your list anything that meets these criteria. Feel free to make the list as long as you want.

Assignment One
A Memory Jogging List
Of Your Most Significant Achievements

---

1) _____

2) _____

3) _____

4) _____

5) _____

6) _____

7) _____

8) _____

9) _____

10) _____

11) _____

12) _____

13) _____

14) _____

15) _____

16) _____

17) _____

18) _____

19) _____

20) _____

OK, now select from this list 10 of the items and write about them *in more detail*. Cover them thoroughly. Your selections should be representative from your whole life, beginning with childhood. Your childhood accomplishments may seem trivial now, but write about them anyway. The important thing is how you felt about them at the time. Put yourself back in time and write about your accomplishments as if they just happened. Recreate the events with the eyes of the person you were at *that* time and in *that* place.

This is an easy task if you follow the guidelines. There are 5 types of information to be included in each detailed recounting of the incident.

First, *state your age* at the time the event took place. Second, *state what happened* in as much detail as you feel necessary to cover the experience thoroughly. Third, *be descriptive* of your feelings. Put all modesty aside. Remember, you are entitled to feel proud of something well done. Fourth, in addition to your feelings, it is essential to know the actions you took which brought about this achievement. *Describe the actions you took* to accomplish what you did. Fifth, *describe the results of those actions.*

The last two items are especially important because a prospective client is basically concerned with two things:

- The actions you took and
- The results of those actions.

You are going to be accepted as a professional based on the skills (future actions) the prospect thinks you might bring to the project and what the results of your skills (future actions) might do for him/her (home owner or agent).

Be sure to select achievements from your list of 20. This is not "busy work". You are trying to discover patterns you have established or are in the process of establishing throughout your life. Everyone has them. When you enjoy doing something, it usually pops up from time to time throughout life, beginning in childhood. Everyone achieves things but not all have a common thread – a common denominator – a similarity in theme or action. It is impossible to look at a couple of achievements and determine your patterns and therefore how you will succeed best in the future.

Landing projects is too important to your business to be taken lightly. One achievement does not make a career, nor should it decide future actions. So you need at least ten significant achievements to get an idea of the direction you should take your business.

Our goal is to help you find that specific direction – your long term success in your business depends on it.

Write only one achievement per page. Take your time. Write as many details as you can remember. It's easier than you think. Be sure to include all five areas: 1) your age; 2) what happened; 3) your feelings; 4) your actions; 5) your results.

Be generous in the amount of time and effort you put into this task. You are preparing yourself to find the precise type of projects you are best suited to execute – the kind that will pay you what you're worth in spite of the going rate in your area.

Chapter Three

New Ways of Thinking

There are four basic myths which home stagers and interior re-designers and decorators accept as being true which need to be dispelled.

Myth No. 1

The first myth is that the consultant doesn't need to work very hard at finding projects – that people will just climb over rooftops to hire them – that the mere existence of a website will bring clients in by the droves. Wrong.

It amazes me how little preparation many consultants give to preparing for a marketing approach and how little time they devote to the actual search. Most people don't like prospecting for clients. Some are timid. Others are willing to settle for just anything. Some think life owes them a living or the good life and that the market should just drop projects right in their lap. Whatever their naïve conception is, the fact is that marketing a business takes work – consistent work.

Myth No. 2

Stagers and re-designers often think that they should be open to any type of project whatever – going out endlessly on free appointments and doing projects for free or for drastic discounts. That's because they haven't really defined what they want and what they don't want. So they wander aimlessly taking anything that comes down the pike, good or bad, and often bad.

It never dawns on them to say "no" – that's not the type of project for me. It never dawns on them that there has to be "a good fit". They don't realize that while a prospect may be sizing them up for hire, they should also be sizing up the prospect to determine if they are the type of people to get involved with in a business dealing of any kind.

Myth No. 3

Inexperienced consultants often think that the prospect holds all the power and control over them, before, during and after a project. Instead of determining how they wish to work, or need to work, they let the homeowner or the agent determine their actions and control the situation.

Most of the time the owner or the agent hasn't a clue about what should be done, how it should be done, when it should be done, or why it should be done. And they don't have a clue as to who should do the work or oversee the project. They rely on their instincts to pick the right person and often purchase the "sizzle" rather than the "steak".

Myth No. 4

Inexperienced consultants think that prospects only hire people who write well or have a good bio or resume. It's important that yours be as good as possible, but prospects are looking for the person who can state their actions and get beneficial results for them and manage the project that needs to be done.

Your prospects are interested in problem solvers – people who act and get results. The goal here, then, is to help you create a portfolio that will show you as an action-minded, result-getting, problem-solving professional.

Give It Top Priority

Begin right now to think of your portfolio development and subsequent search for projects as a *full time job*. Dedicate yourself to giving it every spare minute and hour possible. Even if you're presently getting a project here and there, make this your top priority.

Use your evenings, weekends, lunch hours. Work through your holiday. Skip your vacation. Rest and play time will follow later when your business is buzzing along. Right now you've got to prepare what you need to bring in the business.

Know What You Want

Well known career counselor David Campbell said, "If you don't know where you're going, you'll probably end up somewhere else."

In a few pages you will be learning how to select and substantiate a host of skills that can be used to promote your talents to the fullest. The more skills you can claim and demonstrate, the better your chances are of gaining and keeping the prospect's respect.

You will discover all your skills; you will organize them; you will provide well-documented evidence. You will know who you are more deeply than ever before and you will use that knowledge to your advantage from here on.

You are going to make sure, before you ever accept a project, that it is safe and to your benefit to do so. You will have the confidence of knowing that this project is a good fit for you, that you are a good fit for your client and that both parties have an excellent chance of "winning".

You will select projects on your own and for your own reasons and you will be able to reject certain projects and walk away and not look back.

You will learn to contact only the key individuals – the ones that have the ability to hire you or not – but only for the projects you want. You will not be fitted into any prospect's preconceived slot for you.

You will select who you interview (and consequently be interviewed by). You will refuse to be lost in the shuffle.

Since your projects (that you accept) will be thoroughly screened by you, and because you will have evaluated your prospect fully in advance, you will have the best possible scenario within which to work.

And you'll be happy because you'll know you'll be paid according to the talent you bring to the table. You will conduct your business on your terms and no one else will dictate terms to you.

You will recognize that the person in need of the project the most is the person at the greatest disadvantage. So you will, with security and confidence, avoid wanting any project too much.

You will know that when you turn down one project, another one will take its place, so you will not put yourself into a "compromising" situation that is doomed from the start.

Chapter Four

Keys and Door Bangers

I know you want to be successful. I want you to be successful. But your success requires effort – your effort. You can gather all the information you want, attend seminars, read all my books (and I'll provide you with a good bibliography at the end for further reading), but in the end everything depends on what you are willing to do for yourself about getting your business off the ground.

So now let's spend some time learning some keys to successful client hunting which will keep you on target in your project search.

Key No. 1 – Trust the System

Decide to follow the step-by-step guidelines provided you in this book. They have worked for others and they will work for you too. Don't take short cuts. It's tempting, I know. Don't do it. Do the assignments and complete each one thoroughly before going on to the next. When you have finished, continue to trust and use the system you have created. I'll be giving you more than one way to use your portfolio to gain new clients. It will be up to you to create enough portfolios to circulate around. The more portfolios you create and circulate in and around your community, the more chances you will have of gaining new clients and sub sequent referrals. It has always been a numbers game and it always will be. But you want to lessen the odds whenever possible. So don't make just one portfolio. Make several.

Key No. 2 – Keep At It

Keep at it! Keep at it! Keep at it! The average consultant only contacts six potential prospects in a month or an average of ten in a period of seven weeks. Shocking? Yes. That's not many contacts. Using the system described herein, you will reach many more contacts in a shorter period of time. The more people you reach out to – the more potential projects you will get. It's as simple as that.

But you have to stick with it. Success comes to those who persevere. Don't let discouragement set in and stop you in your tracks. The projects are out there – no matter where you live – there is work out there. You simply have to keep working until you get what you want.

Remember, *this is your life*. This is your business. What is it worth to you? Is it worth an hour or two of your thought and planning? Or is it worth devoting all your energy and available time to secure the best that is out there for you? You decide.

Key No. 3 – Set Your Own Goals

You must *set your own goals*. Decide what you want to do or you will wind up letting someone else make that decision for you. If they make the decision for you, they can do irreparable damage to your self esteem, your self identity and your self satisfaction. And you will probably wind up with the masses of society in a job that just does not suit you – the real you.

Our great God created you with your own special talents, skills and interests which you have developed, perhaps quite unknowingly, as you have grown up and progressed through life. Hopefully you've elected a business that will utilize as many of those God-given talents, skills and interests as possible. Only then will you truly be happy in your work.

In fact, it probably won't even seem like work at all because you'll love every minute of it. I hear this all the time from students. When you love what you're doing, you're going to do a better job of it. When you do a better job, you'll get the happiness, success and fulfillment you're looking for and deserve.

Key No. 4 – Where to Work

It is important for you to decide what you want to do, but also *where you want to work.* How far from your home base or office do you wish to travel? Home staging can involve multiple days, so distance can really become an issue if the project site is far away.

Opportunities are everywhere. People get promoted and move. People get fired and move. People die and the survivors move. People get married and move. People have extra children and move. Children move away and parents move. People tire of their homes and redecorate. People are frustrated and need help.

Problem solvers get hired. That's why you're going to dig deep into your past and find what you've produced to prove you get results. If you take the time to unearth your prospect's problems and you can demonstrate an ability to solve them, you will likely get hired – even if your prospect wasn't thinking of hiring anyone.

Key No. 5 – Reach the Decision Maker

Decide to reach the *decision maker.* The decision maker is the person with the power to hire you. Meeting with a non-decision maker is a waste of time.

Wives are capable of making decisions. But many wives won't make a major decision without discussing it with their husbands. On the other hand, some wives make all the decisions and never consult their husbands. So don't make any assumptions as to who the real decision maker is.

The best way to discover who makes the decisions is to ask. If you're told that major decisions are made by both husband and wife, request a meeting with both of them, not just one or the other.

I make major decisions about my business and on behalf of my family all the time. So it is insulting to me when a vendor assumes that my husband makes the decisions and automatically requires both of us to be present.

You don't want to insult a prospect, so the rule is: Ask!

Resist Being a Door Banger

Those who use these Keys can unlock and enter through the door into the joy and fulfillment waiting beyond. However, those who refuse to use the Keys are those I call "door bangers" because it describes vividly a picture of a person in frustration running like a charging bull trying to smash through an obstacle that is preventing passage and never able to enter into the world of happiness and success on the other side.

Door Banger No. 1 – No Purpose

If you go prospecting with little or no idea of what you want to accomplish, you're not going to be sure you've found it even if you do. You're not even going to know the kind of questions you should ask, let alone feel confident that the project will be awarded to you.

In addition, if you are not focused on a specific goal, it's easy to stray from your path and wind up somewhere you don't belong – perhaps in over your head with no way out. When you have no specific purpose to your prospecting, discouragement, apathy and failure are just around the corner. All three spell disaster for your business.

Door Banger No. 2 – No Plan

Most people set out prospecting using outdated, vague and misleading materials and techniques. They have not properly prepared themselves. They don't even know how to go about it. They have no system nor any organized or comprehensive step-by-step plan.

If they have a portfolio (or even a resume), it is usually filled with nonessential information. At best it might be described as an "obituary" – a brief list of <u>past</u> work, <u>past</u> education, <u>past</u> whatever.

A prospect wants to buy your *future* not your past. While your past is important because it supports your ability to perform in the future, it needs to be presented properly to prospective clients so they will become interested in investing in your future – which is their future as well.

Without a good compass, you will tend to be like a ship floundering in a tormented sea and if you are floundering around hoping miraculously to find port, you will probably end up being lost in the job hunting sea. At best you may wind up in Hawaii when you meant to reach Tokyo.

Door Banger No. 3 – No Will

This is probably the most common consultant's disease. You can read hundreds of papers of advice and acquire all the tools necessary to help you on your way, but you have to decide to move. No one can do it for you. Only you can motivate you. The desire to win comes from within.

Many people are willing to spend thousands of dollars to have someone do it for them. There are times when this makes sense and times when it doesn't. No one can learn your craft except you. You can hire someone to create a website or some other aspect or tool for you, but the talent, the goals, the drive must come from you.

You can hire a company or individual to set up appointments for you, but that can get very expensive. And you will miss out on opportunities to bond with a prospect earlier in the process, whereas your competition might already be on friendly terms with a prospect long before they have their first appointment. That would put you at a tremendous disadvantage, right?

No one can bequeath you motivation, however. That must come from you. You must develop your own internal push each and every day. I can't give it to you; no one can. If you are not motivated to do the assignments and to use the system, it all becomes added information stored in your mental computer or deleted over time. Action is essential. Without action you do not have a business at all.

Door Banger No. 4 – No Time

Do not wait until you are desperate to start. Do not wait until you think you know enough. Do not wait until you have everything created.

Every industry has its cycles. A cycle is determined by the ebb and flow of market interest. For instance, some businesses cater to gift giving, so they have strong cycles just before major holidays, particularly Christmas.

In the home staging business, Christmas is going to be a slow period as people tend not to want to sell their home during the Christmas season. Spring, especially as it nears summer, is a strong season as people want to sell and move during the summer when the kids are out of school.

But if you wait to prospect until summer is upon you, you will miss the lion's share of the cycle. Most people do not decide to hire a consultant the moment they meet one. There is usually a period of meeting, getting acquainted, comparison shopping and so forth before a stager is selected.

Sometimes people don't have a budget or their budget is too low or they can be indecisive for a number of reasons.

No one wants to be rushed or pushed into a decision, so you've got to allow plenty of time to build a relationship, answer questions, plant seeds and water them until they sprout.

If you wait until you feel a bit of desperation, it works against you. Prospects can tell when a consultant feels desperate. There is a greater intensity in your voice and mannerisms. You tend to be too serious and don't have enough fun. Your enthusiasm comes across affected and disingenuous. You might even start to hype your talents and services.

Having to "land" a contract is not a good place to be in. It can cause you to promise what you can't deliver; it can cause you to take on a project that is beyond your skill level or requires more time than you have to give.

Rejections will be unnerving if you need the money to survive. Each interview with a prospect may become more critical, which in turn can make you tense and uneasy and you cease to be yourself. At this point, prospecting becomes difficult and fearful and ineffective, so you stop.

So please don't wait until the pressure is on to start. Do it now.

To sum up, door banging happens even though the Keys are available. The Keys allow access to success minus the heartbreak and headaches. Door banging behavior is especially sad because it is destructive, unnecessary and unproductive. The problem is the behavior and not the door.

All too often the person spends their life blaming everyone and everything and never taking responsibility for their own actions or their destructive actions. The best part is that it is all a choice and you can change past behavior easily by making different choices from here on out.

Set yourself free of self-imposed limitations and defeat by claiming the Keys and using them to your benefit. They will unlock the doors and open up a whole new future for you.

Chapter Five

Pulling Together Your Strengths

Before moving on, be sure to complete Assignment One in Chapter Two. It is important to do the assignments as you move through this manual as they sometimes build on each other and you'll want to refer back to what you have listed. You can write in the manual itself or copy the page and keep your assignments stored in a folder.

Assignment Two
Your Qualities – What You Like About Yourself

Next I want you to list as many attributes as you can that you feel make you someone worthy of being hired for a project. Put yourself in the shoes of your prospect. What kinds of traits would you be seeking if you wanted to hire a home stager or an interior re-designer? Remember, your prospect is buying you and your future.

It is important to try to see yourself from your prospect's perspective as they consider whether or not you meet their criteria for someone they could feel confident in and comfortable hiring for their project. Look closely at your strengths. Begin each sentence with the phrase, "I am a good consultant because . . . ." List a minimum of 25 qualities that make up your personality and character. (Even if it's a quality that only surfaces 10% of the time, it is a part of you and therefore should be included on your list.)

1) I am a good consultant because

2) I am a good consultant because

3) I am a good consultant because

4) I am a good consultant because

5) I am a good consultant because

6) I am a good consultant because

7) I am a good consultant because

8) I am a good consultant because

9) I am a good consultant because

10) I am a good consultant because

11) I am a good consultant because
12) I am a good consultant because

13) I am a good consultant because

14) I am a good consultant because

15) I am a good consultant because

16) I am a good consultant because

17) I am a good consultant because

18) I am a good consultant because

19) I am a good consultant because

20) I am a good consultant because

21) I am a good consultant because

22) I am a good consultant because

23) I am a good consultant because

24) I am a good consultant because

25) I am a good consultant because

Assignment Three
Negative Factors You Can Correct

Now list a few of the things (negative factors) which have been part of your past which are **not** ideal entrepreneurial characteristics. Only list things which you can correct (i.e. If you wish you were taller, or that your feet were smaller, don't note it. You can't do anything to change these conditions, so ignore them.)

I am only concerned with things that you can take actions to *change* in your life. For instance, if you have a habit of being late for an appointment, write it down in the left hand column. In the right hand column, list what actions you will take to change or correct that bad habit (see example).

Here are some more common habits: smoking, lack of follow through, wardrobe deficiencies, overspending, refusal to do these assignments (see I know you're rebelling).

I AM CONCERNED ABOUT:	I WILL CHANGE THIS BY:
Tardiness (sample)	Getting up earlier, preparing my wardrobe and lunch the night before (sample)

I AM CONCERNED ABOUT: **I WILL CHANGE THIS BY:**

You can make copies of this form while it is blank to use to expand your list as needed. When you have changed one of the items and you no longer have this negative habit, cross it off the list and celebrate. It takes work to break a bad habit and you should feel proud whenever you conquer one.

Assignment Four
Your Brief Employment History

List briefly your present and past employment history to give yourself an overview of your experience. Remember, your opinion about this information matters.

1) Employer

Dates of Employment:

Position:

Brief Job Description:

Two of your Most Significant Accomplishments on the Job:

2) Employer

Dates of Employment:

Position:

Brief Job Description:

Two of your Most Significant Accomplishments on the Job:

3) Employer

Dates of Employment:

Position:

Brief Job Description:

Two of your Most Significant Accomplishments on the Job:

4) Employer

Dates of Employment:

Position:

Brief Job Description:

Two of your Most Significant Accomplishments on the Job:

5) Employer

Dates of Employment:

Position:

Brief Job Description:

Two of your Most Significant Accomplishments on the Job:

Chapter Six

Pulling Together Your Biographical Information

Your bio is nothing more than your resume which can include a wide assortment of information, but it should only include information that is pertinent to what you're doing and wanting to accomplish.

So your bio really doesn't need to demonstrate that you have a degree in engineering. It doesn't need to reflect that you were a cheerleader. It doesn't need to prove that you were on a debate team, know how to cook, have animals and hobbies and stuff like that.

But it does need to declare pertinent information such as:

- Your certification designation (if any)
- Length of time in business (unless brand new)
- List of a few of clients (especially if well known in your area)
- Full contact information in a variety of ways (phone, physical address, fax number, email address, website address)
- Your skill sets (more on this in a moment)

- Work history (but only if it relates)
- Educational background (but only if it relates)
- Completed projects, including dates, statistics and outcomes (like: On the market prior to staging for 6 months, sold in 3 weeks with 3 offers higher than original asking price)

Always remember that you are in a design business, so your materials should be well designed and executed. That means your thoughts, even on your bio, should be well organized and positioned to lead the reader in a natural progression.

Don't float sections all over the page. You wouldn't do this if you were staging or redesigning a home, so don't do it on paper or on your website.

Present all material in an orderly, well organized manner, using such graphic elements as bold text, size changes, italics, underlining, boxed text and color to break up the text and make it more readable.

No one wants to read overly long paragraphs. Keep them short and vary their length. Add titles and subtitles to various sections.

No need to make everything a complete sentence, particularly in a resume/bio sheet. You just want to lightly communicate the highlights of your life, background and experience to the prospects.

No one wants to read a book about you, so keep it short and to the point.

Skill Sets

You can literally take skills you have acquired doing totally unrelated tasks and use them to your advantage. And these skills don't even have to be skills you have developed while being paid. If you've never had a job before or never owned a business before, look at the things you do routinely that you feel would apply to the skills of a home stager or re-designer. If they do, claim them, because they are skills you have developed.

Years ago I wrote a book called "The Job Connection". I'm ashamed to admit I never really did anything with it, but I'm going to lift the essence of one of my chapters out and include it here for you.

It's the chapter on targeting your skills and goals.

I want you to look closer at your achievements that you have developed over the course of your life so far. Look for common denominators, similarities in themes and actions, which will all form behavior patterns in order to identify major areas where you have performed brilliantly and the ways you commonly relate to other people.

Look at what you have done in the past that was successful. By recognizing them, and focusing just on them, and then repeating them in the staging and redesign industry, you will find success much easier to attain.

I have coined a couple of phrases that state, "Profit Follows Passion" or "Profits Follow Passion". If you can take what you have been successful doing in the past and translate that over to our industry, you will have the best possible chance to be happy and successful in your work.

Motivational Thrust

Everyone has **one motivational thrust** – something they hope to get through their accomplishments. Although accomplishments vary, the motivation that prompted them in the first place generally remains constant. For instance, perhaps you are always seeking recognition from others, or perhaps you are motivated by a need to serve and help others, or perhaps you want to acquire possessions.

In order to focus on your motivational thrust, you now need to refer back to Assignment No. 1 and expand on it. For our purposes now, divide your life into 10 different stages beginning from your youth until today. Then write down 10 accomplishments from Assignment No. 1, choosing some from each stage of life. From this pool of lifetime achievements, it will be easy to pick up a pattern – as you look for your motivational thrusts.

You should find that one or two, at least, from the list below will surface in common throughout your whole life. These are the most common motivational thrusts, adapted from (*The Truth About You,* Arthur F. Miller and Ralph T. Mattson):

- Acquire/Possess
- Discover/Learn
- Gain Recognition/Honors
- Master/Perfect
- Pioneer/Explore
- Develop/Build/Structure
- Make the Grade/Fulfill Requirements
- Be in Charge/Command
- Excel/Be the Best
- Improve/Do Better
- Overcome/Combat
- Serve/Help
- Gain Response/Gratitude
- Shape/Influence Control

Operating with People

Usually you seek out a *particular role or relationship with other people.* Your role may vary depending on the people you are with and the circumstances you find yourself in, or perhaps you are the same with all people. First take a look at the pronouns you have used in writing your accomplishments. Do you mostly use the first person "I" in describing what was accomplished? Or do you often use collective words like "we" or "us"?

Those who generally talk in the first person ("I") are more likely to be individualists, while those who often use "we" or "us" tend to be team members. Perhaps you are an individualist in some circumstances and a group member in others. In the staging and redesign business, it is important to be an individualist who is a self starter, can go it alone when needed, who is a *take charge* person. Sell that to your prospects as an asset.

On the other hand, being a team player is important too, especially if you're bringing in vendors to provide services, when you're working in concert with a real estate agent as well as the homeowner, or if you have one or more partners in your business. Sell that as an asset you have and that your goal is to be a 3-part, 4-part, 5-part team (and so on) for the purpose of getting that house sold quickly and for top dollar.

Know how you function best and most comfortably. Your work will require you to work alone and it will bring you into contact with other people. Understanding how you function best with regard to other people will help you present these qualities in your portfolio. Following are some categories which can help you relate to others:

Team Member
Wants to be with one or more other persons

Individualist
Wants a defined role and prefers to get results without having to rely on others

Team Leader
Can lead others but wants also to be involved in the action

Director
Wants others to do things exactly their own way

Coordinator
Likes to be at the hub of the action and gets a variety of other people's efforts involved when necessary

Coach
Wants to help others develop their talent or improve their knowledge

Manager
Wants to get results by managing the talents of others

It is important to note whether your preferred role changes when you are in the company of authority figures, clients or prospects as opposed to when you are in the company of your family, your pastor, the police, or vendors.

You may discover you're an individualist when alone but a director when you're in a group. It is important to ascertain the way you are most comfortable in your relationship to a real estate agent, the home owner, your vendors, people you like instantly, and people you dislike instantly. This will help you know whether you want to take on a project or pass it up.

Using Certain Abilities

One of the most vital steps to landing that project is *discovering your motivational abilities.* A first clue will come from noting the *verbs* you chose when writing down your accomplishments. Verbs carry the action and demonstrate which types of actions you often take to achieve your goals. Most people have five to seven motivational abilities, so look for a variety.

You may have more, but look for the most prominent in your life. If a project requires you to use your other abilities, it does not mean you will fail, only that you may find them more difficult to do.

Discovering your strongest abilities – the ones you generally feel confident using – will help you accept projects where these abilities can be exercised to the fullest. You'll discover the work is perfectly suited for you.

Having already developed these abilities (proven by your past achievements), you should find the tasks and responsibilities of the project to be relatively easy to accomplish, because you are using your strongest skills.

Here is a list of some of the most common abilities – a combination of which are found in most projects you may come across:

- Administer /Maintain
- Build / Develop
- Convince /Persuade
- Design / Draw
- Formulate / Theorize
- Learn / Study
- Make Friends /Build Relations
- Operate /Run
- Perform /Entertain
- Practice /Perfect
- Synthesize /Harmonize
- Write /Communicate
- Analyze /Evaluate
- Control /Schedule
- Create /Shape
- Do /Execute
- Innovate /Improvise
- Nurture /Nurse
- Observe /Comprehend

- Organize
- Plan
- Research /Experiment
- Teach /Train

Rules for Adding Up Your Success Patterns for Your Bio

Here are some quick rules to follow when you are studying your list of accomplishments and looking at each achievement and scoring them for relevance.

1. Do not try to interpret the words. Simply note which ones jump out at you and which ones do not.
2. Do not jump to conclusions (just because you are good at one thing, doesn't mean you are automatically good at another one)
3. Do not try to figure out "why" a certain action was taken in the past. Do not try to evaluate your actions; simply add the skill to your list of skill sets.
4. Do not judge your actions. You are not to condemn or approve them, simply to add them to your list.
5. Look for actions that pop up throughout your whole lifetime. You're looking for a pattern. Patterns are established when they pop up several times throughout your life, not just once.
6. Do not force an action to be there if it is not included in that particular achievement. Stay as objective as possible.
7. Enjoy these discoveries about yourself.

To do this properly you must write down your achievement on paper, describing in story-like fashion what happened, being as detailed as possible about every phase: the goal, the steps taken to achieve the goal, and the results of the actions.

Here is a list of skills (more than you'll ever need), which I feel important for a consultant to have to greater or lesser degree, listed in alphabetical order. Rate each in order of frequency on a scale of 1-15 (15 being a very strong skill and 1 being a very low skill). Put the assigned number out to the side of the skill, left of the bullet.

Assignment Five
Identifying Your Skill Sets

- Accentuating
- Accessorizing
- Accounting
- Achieving
- Acquiring
- Acting on behalf of
- Adapting
- Addressing
- Adjusting
- Administering
- Administrating
- Advertising
- Advising
- Aiding
- Allocating
- Analyzing
- Answering
- Anticipating
- Applying
- Appraising
- Approving
- Arbitrating
- Arranging
- Articulating
- Ascertaining

- Assembling
- Assessing
- Assigning
- Attaining
- Attending
- Attracting
- Auditing
- Balancing
- Bargaining
- Beautifying
- Bidding
- Binding
- Bookkeeping
- Briefing
- Bringing
- Brokering
- Budgeting
- Building
- Calculating
- Caring
- Carrying
- Causing
- Charting
- Checking
- Clarifying

- Classifying
- Cleaning
- Clearing
- Climbing
- Coaching
- Collaborating
- Collating
- Collecting
- Color coordinating
- Coloring
- Comforting
- Commenting
- Communicating
- Comparing
- Competing
- Compiling
- Composing
- Comprising
- Computing
- Conceiving
- Conceptualizing
- Conducting
- Confiding
- Constructing
- Consulting
- Contacting
- Contracting
- Contributing
- Controlling
- Conversing
- Conveying
- Cooking
- Cooperating
- Coordinating
- Copying
- Correcting
- Costing
- Counseling
- Counting
- Crafting
- Creating
- Critiquing
- Cultivating
- Curing
- Customizing
- Cutting
- Debating
- Dealing
- Decluttering
- Deciding
- Decision-making
- Decorating
- De-emphasizing
- Defining
- Delegating
- Delivering
- Demonstrating
- Depersonalizing
- Describing
- Designing
- Detailing
- Detecting
- Developing
- Diagramming
- Directing
- Discovering
- Discussing
- Dispatching
- Dissecting
- Diverting
- Doing
- Drafting

- Drawing
- Driving
- Economizing
- Editing
- Educating
- Effecting
- Embellishing
- Empathizing
- Employing
- Empowering
- Enabling
- Encouraging
- Energizing
- Enforcing
- Enhancing
- Enlightening
- Enlisting
- Envisioning
- Establishing
- Estimating
- Evaluating
- Examining
- Executing
- Exercising
- Expediting
- Experimenting
- Explaining
- Exploring
- Exposing
- Expressing
- Extracting
- Facilitating
- Fashioning
- Feeling
- Figuring
- Filing
- Filling
- Financing
- Finding
- Firing
- Fitting
- Fixing
- Focusing
- Following
- Following-thru
- Forecasting
- Foreseeing
- Forging
- Formatting
- Forming
- Formulating
- Fostering
- Gathering
- Generating
- Getting
- Getting Things Done
- Giving
- Grafting
- Graphing
- Grounds-keeping
- Grouping
- Growing
- Guiding
- Handcrafting
- Handling
- Hearing
- Helping
- Hiring
- Home staging
- Hostessing
- Humanizing

- Human Relating
- Humoring
- Idea Forming
- Identifying
- Illustrating
- Imagining
- Implementing
- Impressing
- Improving
- Informing
- Individualizing
- Influencing
- Initiating
- Innovating
- Inquiring
- Inspecting
- Inspiring
- Installing
- Instilling
- Instructing
- Integrating
- Internet marketing
- Interpreting
- Interviewing
- Inventing
- Investing
- Invoicing
- Isolating
- Joking
- Judging
- Justifying
- Keeping
- Landscaping
- Laying
- Leading
- Learning

- Lecturing
- Liasoning
- Lifting
- Lighting
- Listening
- Machining
- Maintaining
- Making
- Managing
- Manifesting
- Manipulating
- Mapping
- Marketing
- Measuring
- Mechanizing
- Mediating
- Memorizing
- Mentoring
- Merging
- Mobilizing
- Modeling
- Modifying
- Molding
- Motivating
- Moving
- Navigating
- Negotiating
- Networking
- Noting
- Nursing
- Nurturing
- Observing
- Obtaining
- Operating
- Ordering
- Organizing

- Overseeing
- Owning
- Painting
- Perceiving
- Performing
- Persevering
- Persuading
- Photographing
- Placing
- Planning
- Planting
- Playing
- Policy-making
- Practicing
- Preparing
- Presenting
- Pressing
- Prioritizing
- Problem-solving
- Processing
- Producing
- Programming
- Projecting
- Promoting
- Promotional-writing
- Proofreading
- Positioning
- Public speaking
- Publicizing
- Publishing
- Pulling
- Purchasing
- Pushing
- Putting
- Qualifying
- Quizzing
- Reading
- Rearranging
- Reasoning
- Reassigning
- Recognizing
- Recommending
- Reconciling
- Recording
- Recordkeeping
- Recreating
- Recruiting
- Redecorating
- Redesigning
- Reducing
- Re-evaluating
- Referring
- Reflecting
- Relating
- Remembering
- Removing
- Rendering
- Renegotiating
- Reorganizing
- Repairing
- Reporting
- Repositioning
- Representing
- Reproducing
- Repurposing
- Responding
- Researching
- Restoring
- Retrieving
- Reviewing
- Running

- Scanning
- Scheduling
- Screening
- Seeing
- Selecting
- Self-motivating
- Selling
- Sensitizing
- Servicing
- Setting Up
- Serving
- Shaping
- Sharing
- Shipping
- Shopping
- Showing
- Simplifying
- Sizing Up
- Socializing
- Solidifying
- Solving
- Space planning
- Speaking
- Speech-writing
- Staging
- Stimulating
- Structuring
- Studying
- Styling
- Subcontracting
- Summarizing
- Surveying
- Switching
- Symbolizing
- Synthesizing
- Systematizing

- Tabulating
- Tackling
- Taking
- Talking
- Teaching
- Team building
- Teaming
- Telephoning
- Tending
- Testing
- Theorizing
- Thinking
- Tracing
- Training
- Translating
- Tracking
- Traveling
- Treating
- Trouble shooting
- Typing
- Understanding
- Upgrading
- Unloading
- Uploading
- Updating
- Using
- Utilizing
- Validating
- Verbalizing
- Visualizing
- Wallpapering
- Washing
- Watching over
- Weaving
- Winning
- Wording

- Working
- Writing

- Other _____
- Other_____

Whew! That's a pretty exhausting list and you're sure to find many skills listed that you can easily claim as part of your overall skill set.

Now list all of the skills you've assigned a #15. These are your strongest, most prominent skills and the ones you will focus on first. Then list the #14, #13, #12 skills and so on. The skills that you ranked lowest will be the ones you'll skip as far as your portfolio is concerned. You'll, of course, be listing your strongest skills in your bio.

Substantiating Your Claims

It's not enough to just list your skills. You want to give examples of what you accomplished that gives evidence that you do, indeed, have that skill. Of course it's best if your evidence (short 2-3 sentence example) is related to our industry. Those are the most powerful.

If, however, none of your accomplishments to date have anything to do with decorating, staging, real estate or redesign, perhaps they have to do with construction, advertising, appraising and such. Loosely related industries can also help substantiate your claims.

If desperate, use examples from general life experience. Having something to substantiate your claim is better than nothing at all.

Listing Your Education

Again, list only the education that will apply to our industry. You need not list high school or below. Everyone assumes you graduated from high school. (The exception to this might be where you list your favorite courses in Assignment Six.

If you have a degree in interior design or a real estate license, or a membership in any prestigious associations, and affiliations, by all means list them.

List where you got your certification, if you have one, and below that (if certified by my company), be sure to state that your qualifications demanded passage of an exam and the submission of a top notch portfolio. This will lift your credentials way up above all other designations in the home staging and redesign industries, in my opinion, because you had to prove you had the talent before gaining your designation.

If you have won any awards, attending seminars, been published in newspapers or magazines, be sure to mention those. Make copies of any clippings to include as well.

If you're actively participating in my free online discussion forum, and have achieved a Silver, Gold or Diamond Level, be sure to inform them of the Forum, where they can go to see that you are indeed an "expert" by the number and quality of your posts. You could even make a screen capture of a page of your posts and print off a copy to include.

If you haven't been there yet and joined, here is the link: **http://www.decorate-redecorate.com/smf** I ask you not to come just to read, but to join and add your questions and contribute for the good of everyone. Be a giver, not a taker. This is the only *free* on-line discussion that I presently know about devoted to our industries.

A brief Mission Statement or Statement of your Goals can also be included. It is not necessary to list your age, height or weight, nor your marital status and hobbies. Don't clog up your Bio with unnecessary stuff.

And if you feel any part of these suggestions are not areas where you can excel, then leave them out altogether (with the exception of your skill set). Everyone – and I do mean everyone – has skills, whether they recognize them yet or not.

Now we're going to spend some quality time looking at your educational background and history. While all education is important, and I believe you can never have too much, there will be some aspects of your education that will not have much or any application to our industry.

As such, it becomes useless and harmful to include it in your bio. But in order to decide what needs to be included and what needs to be dropped out, I want you to work on the next Assignment so you'll be able to tell at a glance where your strengths lie and where you might have some weaknesses.

So please do not dismiss this portion as non-essential. Do all of the assignments I give you to achieve the best results.

Personal and Family Information

I used to think that this type of information was not needed but I have since changed my mind. Add a page or two about your personal life, show pictures of your family, your pets, you busy doing one of your favorite hobbies. People may or may not be interested in such information, but there will be a segment of people who will want to relate to you in some more personal manner. As you have opportunity to build a friendship with your prospects, and then your clients, you may discover that some people hired you because you were from the same home town, or graduated from the same high school, or because you love dogs or cats the way they do.

Or they may see pictures of your kids who are the same age as theirs. It can be anything at all that helps you reach some common ground and gets you hired in the end.

Assignment Six
Your Educational History

Formal Education
Institution & Dates   Major Areas of Study

Informal Education
This list should include skills you have taught yourself, skills taught you by others, private studies, military training, employer-sponsored seminars, on-the-job training, home study courses, books read, etc.

Your Favorite Courses
Begin in grade school and continue through your formal and informal schooling.

Your Favorite Hobbies
What do you enjoy doing most?

Awards, Special Talents Not Mentioned Earlier
(foreign languages, trophies, etc.)

Your Financial Goals
My greatest earnings were in _____ (year).

I earned $_____.

This year I am earning $_____ (approximately).

Five years from now I anticipate earning $_____
per year.

Ten years from now I anticipate earning $_____
per year.

Your Motivational Success Factors
Go back to your Success Factors assignment and list all
categories which scored six or more points.

Now take these factors and group them in similar categories whenever possible (i.e. teaching, training, public speaking are all similar and might be grouped together).

GROUP 1

GROUP 2

GROUP 3

GROUP 4

GROUP 5

GROUP 6

GROUP 7

GROUP 8

GROUP 9

Now let's focus on common categories even more. Make groupings of similar success factor skills where you have six or more points assigned. In the following list of similar groupings which describe many typical responsibilities, pick out three areas you would most want to emphasize and feel would enhance your business enjoyment.

- Help people, be of service
- Create, imagine, develop, invent
- Decorate, organize, rearrange
- Work independently, own/collect things
- Count, keep records, calculate
- Design, color, shape things
- Foresight, ideas, goals
- Persuade, sell, influence others
- Research, systematize, analyze
- Build, assemble, fix
- Clean, refresh, spruce up
- Read, write, talk, speak, teach
- Observe, inspect, operate
- Direct or manage others
- Outdoors, travel activities
- Perform, demonstrate, seminars, speak

Arrange the groups of skills in accordance with their importance to you:

First Group:

Second Group:

Third Group:

Your ideal business makeup should incorporate the defined and selected skill groupings to the fullest. If it does, you now have the perfect objective to state on your bio and to begin your project searches. If it does not include your selected skill groupings listed above, you may be in the wrong business and might not enjoy your work as much as you should and could.

Pulling It All Together

There are several reasons for writing a good bio. The most obvious is that it provides you with a visual document in addition to your physical presence. Your past achievements, which are strong indications of your future achievements, are documented on a paper which will stay with your prospect long after you have left their home or office. It will continue to speak well for you. People are predisposed to accept written facts more readily than spoken words, so your bio enhances and enforces your verbal presentation.

In addition, your bio presents your objective and the facts supporting it in a positive way. Your assets are what is most interesting to a prospective client. Your bio, if presented properly, will prove that your objective is realistic because of your supporting statements.

You will also keep your prospect from having to wade through unrelated subject matter which has little bearing on the project you are seeking to manage for them.

Your bio can also serve as a conversation starter to get the interview process off the ground. You can use it as a point of reference and as a script to keep the meeting going in the direction you wish it to go.

Remember, you are there looking to offer your services but you're also interviewing the prospect to determine if the project will be a good fit for all parties involved.

The First Draft

The first draft is the first writing. Don't worry about final format. Your purpose is to build a compelling case. It is vital that you make factual statements which you can substantiate. The statements you make should help your prospect understand that you are qualified to handle the project. After you have finished the first draft, you will begin editing it – building and formatting the final edition.

After the First Draft

After you've pulled together your information and compiled it on no more than 1-2 pages, give it to a few people you know who are highly successful people and ask them to critique it.

Ask them to tell you where they feel it is strong and where they feel it is weak. Listen to what they say. If several people make the same observation, whether good or bad, then you have a consensus of opinion. Pay attention and adjust to any consensus you get.

But if only one person comments on an area that the rest do not, you'll have to weigh the strength of their comment and whether you feel adjustment is needed or not.

Summarizing Your Bio

In summary, your Bio should contain most if not all of the following ingredients:

- Your picture
- Your contact information
- Your qualifications
- Your achievements and supporting evidence
- Your experience

- Your education
- Other related information such as your family, pets, awards, hobbies and the like

After the first two above, include a section ONLY if you have something good to include that relates to the home staging and redesign industry.

You'll be tempted to want to put every glorious attribute down on the list. Refrain from doing that. If an area is weak, your prospect will wonder why it's there and weakness makes them ask questions and then you have to defend yourself. Better to not have it included than to have it generate negative comments or arouse suspicions.

Here is a mantra I try hard to live by: "When in doubt, don't." If you're not sure, that's a pretty good indication that you should probably leave it out.

Chapter Seven

Writing Copy That Sells

Happily, for most of us who are not professional writers, George Orwell once wrote, "The defense of the English language . . . has nothing to do with correct grammar and syntax, which are of no importance so long as one makes one's meaning clear . . . though it does imply using the fewest and shortest words that will cover one's meaning. What is above all needed is to let the meaning choose the word, and not the other way around. . . . I have not here been considering the literary use of language, but merely language as an instrument for expressing and not for concealing or preventing thought."

You're not going to get an English lesson nor will you get a writing lesson from me. I'm not qualified to give you either one, to be sure. Having spent the bulk of my junior and senior high school years attending a Canadian school, my spelling is no doubt different from yours. I've tried to catch these differences and change them to the spelling of Americans, but I'm sure some have escaped the editor's bullet and you'll find a few still exist in this manual. But what you will get, hopefully, is some guidance into how to write some type of copy that will get your message across and perhaps even inspire someone to call you or send you an email.

President Bush is known for having trouble completing an off-the-cuff thought and his grammar and syntax is often a mess. But he sold the country on making him President and on entering the Iraq war none-the-less, whether you agree now with his decisions or not.

While he butchers words and pronounces some words incorrectly, he is able to make his meaning clear, unlike other politicians who have been superior speakers but did not reach the highest office in the country.

Good communication requires conviction and authenticity. It does not require a vast vocabulary nor perfect grammar.

Here, by the way, are some language rules that Orwell laid out. Each point is sound writing advice, whether I followed the rules or not (George Orwell, *Politics and the English Language):*

1. Never use a metaphor, simile, or other figure of speech which you are used to seeing in print.
2. Never use a long word where a short one will do.
3. If it is possible to cut a word out, always cut it out.
4. Never use the passive when you can use the active.
5. Never use a foreign phrase, a scientific word, or a jargon word if you can think of an everyday English equivalent.
6. Break any of these rules sooner than say anything outright barbarous.

So the important thing is *not* that your writing style be perfect, but that you be able to get your meaning across to your readers in as simple and efficient a means as possible.

People often say that when they read my books that it feels as if I'm talking directly to them. What that means is that my style feels personal to them.

This makes me very happy as it is exactly what I'm striving to accomplish. My syntax is not perfect. My grammar is not perfect. My spelling is not perfect. I'm the first to admit that.

But apparently most people feel comfortable reading what I write and the majority are able to grasp the meaning I'm trying to convey.

So don't feel fearful when you sit down to compose copy for your cover letter, your brochure, your bio sheet or whatever else you decide to include in your portfolio. Be yourself. Be genuine and enthusiastic and the rest will take care of itself.

But just to back yourself up, when you finish writing your copy, give it to a trusted friend or relative to read, edit, correct. Notice I said "trusted" person. They should be someone who demonstrates already the ability to communicate effectively. The main thing you will want to know is if they are able to grasp your meaning. If not, then go back to your desk and improve what you've written until your meaning is easy to understand.

21st Century Words

Words change over time and so do their meanings. Some words are considered "in" and others wind up tossed aside as "dated". While you'll tend to use words that are common to your lifestyle and where you live, there are some specific words I want you to consider that have risen up in today's business climate as being particularly thought provoking.

You do want your copy to be effective in today's marketplace and so I'm going to give you a list of words and phrases that have proven effective recently as of this writing. Try to incorporate some of these into your writing so that you are perceived as being contemporary in your style and approach.

Imagine   Lifestyle
Hassle-free   Accountability

Results	Investment
Can-Do Spirit	Casual elegance
Innovation	Independent
Renew,	Peace of mind
Revitalize	Certified
Rejuvenate	All-American
Restore	Prosperity
Rekindle	Spirituality
Reinvent	Financial security
Efficient	A "balanced approach"
Efficiency	A culture of
The Right to . . .	Straight talk
Client-centered	Change

Often the words you choose to use can make a huge difference in the perceived value your prospect or client will gather from your ideas and concepts. I can remember when a second-hand car was called a "used car". Today, however, those cars are called "pre-owned vehicles". See what I mean?

Pre-owned doesn't sound as bad as "used", right?

11 Rules for Success

No matter what you're going to write for your portfolio, here are ten simple rules to follow that will place you on solid ground as a writer.

1. Keep it simple. Use small words. The average American did not graduate from college and might not know the difference between the word *effect* and the word *affect*. Short words are easier to read and to skim – and yes, people will skim what you write no matter how clever you think you put pen to paper. Don't think I don't know you're skimming my book too, you rascal.
2. Keep it short. Don't write long, belabored paragraphs. Don't write sentences that go on and on and on. Many people get caught up in the overuse of connective

words such as *"and"*. Don't forget that there are punctuation marks such as a period, a comma or a semi-colon (or even a dash).

3. Establish credibility. People need to believe what you're saying. If you exaggerate, or lack sincerity, or you use erroneous facts, your words will lack impact. Words take on a life of their own, but they also truly represent you and you represent your words. Don't over promise or make promises can't keep or don't intend to keep.

4. Be consistent. Use headlines, sub-headlines, captions, slogans and so forth repeatedly. Many companies have catapulted themselves into the hearts of people for generations by continuously repeating the same slogan over and over again. For instance, what company says, "What can Brown do for you?" Or who said, "The breakfast of champions" or "When you care enough to send the very best"?

5. Offer something new and different. Don't use the same offers your competition uses. Be original. Define an old idea in a new way. Use newer words. Go where no one has gone before with your words and phrases. If your opportunity is really new and different, it will attract attention, grab interest and get people to participate. You'll know when you have it when you start to get comments like, "I didn't know that".

6. The mental and verbal sounds matter. A string of words that have the same sound or are similar can be very memorable – you know the kind I mean that have a poetic ring to them. Remember "Snap, Crackle, and Pop"? You can just "hear" the sounds that the words convey.

7. Use aspiration. One of the reasons Barack Obama is so popular right now is that he says the things that people *want* to hear in his speeches. His speeches are filled with statements of hope, and people respond to that. Humanize your message with stories which will trigger emotional responses from your readers. When your readers can see themselves in your stories and

can perceive a genuine benefit and value for themselves by hiring you, then why wouldn't they hire you? Give them a vision of the type of person they will become after using your services. Show them a better life that they have been wishing to have which your service will help them attain.

8. Use visualization. Use descriptive verbs and adjectives and paint a vivid picture for your prospect. This is one of the reasons the word "imagine" is so powerful today. When you can get your reader to see them selves enjoying the benefits of your service, you've achieved a whole lot.

9. Ask plenty of questions. Southwest Airlines asks the question, "Want to get away?" after showing you someone getting themselves into an embarrassing situation. Verizon Wireless asks you, "Can you hear me now?" The milk campaign asks, "Got milk?" Why not try something like, "Are you better off selling your home for $10,000 less than you need to?" Or try "Are you satisfied living in a home you're ashamed to show visitors?" "Will your home make your mother in law jealous or critical of you?" (Wow. That should make them react!) Asking a rhetorical question makes the reader's reaction personal – and personalization is the best communication you'll ever use.

10. Make your message relevant and in full context. You're going to need to give people the "why" of your message before you give them the path to success. You've got to establish context before you present results. If your reader doesn't understand where you're coming from and what you're talking about, they won't care if there is a solution or not. But that's only half the battle. Your message must be relevant to them or they'll tune you out as well. Know what matters to your prospect and frame your message around what matters to them or it is a wasted message.

11. Images matter. Background images and illustrations are very powerful in communicating your message.

Make sure your images are suitable for all readers and are relevant to the message where they are placed. It's not all about words and meanings that you intend. But it's all about what your reader "hears" and "sees" – it's all about how your message is interpreted.

Using Cover Letters

There are many methods consultants use to hunt for clients. Some methods are a waste of time. I'll be dealing with those that are successful techniques. But this method is not for the weak or the lazy. It's a method that high paid executives use when looking for a career position with a company. But they can also be used by you, the consultant.

This is not a door-to-door method. It is not a sales method for an idea or invention. It's not the typical methods you might learn elsewhere. It's called the *referral method.* This method is to get you going so that no matter who you are, and no matter where you live, you should be able to get your business off the ground and begin the process of looking for clients.

The referral method of interviewing is often called *networking* by professionals, for it is a system of multiplying your chances for landing a project for yourself through other people. This successful technique puts you in touch with key decision makers who have the power to hire you or can use their power to move you closer to other decision makers until you meet one interested in your services (your future actions and the results of those actions).

You must first make contact with key individuals you currently know. Once your portfolio is completed, you will research and select the key decision makers from your list that you currently know and that's where you'll start.

Your Best Contacts

Following is a work sheet where you can begin filling in the names of professionals and homeowners you already know in various fields whom you can contact. You will be writing first to people you know who are successful in their fields and, of course, own homes.

You will start with people you know because you'll probably feel more comfortable than with a stranger and you'll find it easier to get an appointment with them. Friends are safe. Friends are comfortable. So start with them.

If you sit down and give this serious thought, you should be amazed at how many professionals you actually know. Whether you know the person well or not, you'll start with a letter to set up an appointment. Don't skip the letter writing stage as the process is more effective when used.

Most people are willing to give you a little of their time, especially when they are not worried that you're trying to sell them something. The whole approach I'm teaching you is to ask for something that they can give you freely and without hesitation.

That something is advice.

Everyone loves to give advice whether they will admit it or not. We all love to be thought of as people with wisdom. So it's a compliment to be asked for one's opinion. Later I'll cover the type of letter you will send. For now, fill out the worksheet following and get ready to use it when the time comes.

As you get further into preparing your portfolio, I'll discuss some other ideas of how to use it in addition to the referral method I'm discussing right now.

Assignment Seven
Your Best Contacts

PERSON TO CONTACT
COMPANY, HOME ADDRESS, PHONE, EMAIL

PRESENT/FORMER EMPLOYERS	
BANKERS/FINANCE	
ACCOUNTANTS	
DOCTORS/DENTISTS CHIROPRACTORS	
LAWYERS	
CLERGY	

POLITICIANS/ CIVIC LEADERS	
FORMER BUSINESS ASSOCIATES	
SALES PERSONS	
COLLEGE PRESIDENTS/ PROFESSORS/TEACHERS	
SOCIAL CLUBS/ ALUMNI ASSOCIATIONS	
FRIENDS/ RELATIVES	
NEIGHBORS	
CONSULTANTS	

REAL ESTATE AGENTS/ BROKERS	
INSURANCE AGENTS	
BUSINESS OWNERS OR EXECUTIVES	
OTHERS	

Give a good amount of time to constructing this list because it is your core contact group from which you should derive a large amount of advice and referrals – and possibly some business projects as well.

Your goal is to eventually get projects which utilize your strongest abilities, which interest you, which allow you to function in a comfortable setting and which provide you maximum opportunity for growth, advancement, profit, prestige, fulfillment and happiness.

Chapter Eight

The Referral Letter

Whenever you write a letter, it is important to follow some basic rules. These rules will also apply to your cover letter that you'll want to include in the actual portfolio.

1. Be sure to make your letters sincere, warm and personal. It is important the reader responds positively to what you write.
2. Don't use worn-out stereotype phrases. Be original and personable, not flip, nor too casual. It is a business letter and should reflect that aura.
3. Use a nice textured white or off-white stationery, unless you have well designed, business letterhead.
4. Use a business size envelope (No. 10), preferably one that matches the color and texture of your paper.
5. Type the letter and the envelope using your computer and printer. If you don't have a computer and printer, go to the library and rent one or ask a friend if you can use their computer.

Never hand write this letter or anything else unless you are looking for extra incentive for it to be opened and read, and by that I mean, only the envelope could be handwritten (never the letter). When I mail out my brochures to prospective students, I hand write their name and address, but these are people who have already been exposed to my training by virtue of a free ebook they registered for and they are receiving a professionally designed and printed brochure. Keep your letters brief and to the point – preferably one page in length. Remember, the only goal of the letter is to let them know that you will follow up to set an appointment. More on this in a bit. Make a copy of your letter for future reference and keep notes on when specific letters were mailed out.

6. Don't include your bio or anything else with the letter. You'll be taking your portfolio with you on the appointment (which will include your bio).

The opening statement in your letter should be warm, friendly and sincere, explaining your purpose in writing to that particular individual.

If you already know the person, your salutation can be more informal. But if you don't know the person, keep the salutation formal.

If you were referred by someone else, begin by saying, "Mr. A suggested I write you . . ."

If this is a "blind" letter (in other words, writing to someone without a referral whom you don't know), you might begin, "I am writing to you . . . because of your position . . . " or you can start, ". . . because of your expertise in . . ."

Briefly explain your present situation, your objective and your need for advice and direction. Everyone likes to give advice and be considered an *expert,* so they will have a natural tendency to be willing to see you. You're also asking for something that costs them nothing to give, so they won't be putting up any barriers.

Following I'll include a sample letter to give you an idea. Feel free to take ideas from it but be sure to word your letter in phraseology that is comfortable and natural for you. Your letter should reflect your own unique personality and circumstances, not mine. These samples are given just to give you a guideline; they are not meant to be copied verbatim.

Your Name
Your Business Name
Your Business Address
Your Business Phone, Email
Your Website Name

Date

Name of Your Contact
Name of Your Contact's Company (if any)
Street Address of the Company or Home Address (contact's)
City, State and Zip Code (contact's)

Dear _____:

I am writing you because I'm seeking your advice as someone with a proven track record, expertise and success in your (field, company, neighborhood, city).

I'm considering a "second" career since (quitting my previous job, retiring, or whatever you've been doing). I miss the challenge of decision-making and problem-solving, and the gratification of being a part of the process of making a difference and seeing things change for the better.

In other words, I want to get back in the "game" and affiliate with people who share similar goals.

The stimulating aspect of this part of my search is that I'm completely open to any advice and suggestions that come my way.

This brings me to this letter and how you might be able to give me some important guidance.

I'm seeking a brief meeting with you (not more than 11 minutes) to ask your advice regarding my new contemplated direction. This is **not** a request for employment. On the contrary, this is a request for help with my research regarding the options before me.

I'm very aware that this request may appear presumptuous on my part – but having been on your side of this kind of request in the past, I have experienced satisfaction personally and professionally from having been someone's short-term trusted advisor, and I trust the same would be true for you also, if you are so kind as to grant me a brief meeting.

Being aware of the importance of your time, I will bring a portfolio of my background and experience, which should minimize the time needed for a meaningful exchange between us.

Your consideration will be appreciated. I will call your office in a few days regarding an appointment convenient to your schedule.

Sincerely,

Make it clear that you are not expecting the recipient of your letter to offer you a job or give you anything that costs them something. The last thing you want to do is to make this person feel uncomfortable or pressured in any way. No one likes to say "no", so it is important that you clearly state in your letter that *you are not asking for a job*, but simply for their advice and suggestions. Advice is something they can give you, if they have the time.

Of course time is the vital issue. You will be writing busy people whose time is not only limited, but valuable. So be sure to express your appreciation in the letter for any time that is granted you, recognizing this is a limited and valuable commodity.

State that you will not need a great deal of time, but would appreciate a short interview which will enable you to seek their advice and direction. You should be specific and might suggest some of the following areas for discussion:

- Your objective as stated in your portfolio (which you will take with you);
- Your overall presentation of yourself;
- Your plans to market yourself;
- The individuals/companies/organizations your executive feels you should contact next;

- The future trends visualized by the executive in your new chosen field.

Never ask the executive for anything other than a brief meeting. Take all the initiative yourself and do not ask this person to phone you. Advise them that you will call in a few days to set up a brief, convenient appointment. It is your responsibility to initiate the call and set up the appointment if you want to have the interview. Keeping the initiative also prevents you from taking more of their time than is necessary.

In writing the draft of your first letter, try to fill two pages. It is much easier to edit and eliminate copy than it is to create more copy once the letter is composed. State your circumstances concisely. The letter should reflect your own particular situation, because if it is so general that it would apply to a number of other people, it is not personal enough and therefore not a powerful letter. This letter should speak only about you.

You may need to write several drafts before you feel your letter includes the necessary information about you in a personal, warm (yet businesslike) manner. Read the letter to friends to get their reactions. You cannot be as objective as someone else, so utilize their help as much as possible whenever you can. Don't get angry if you get some criticism. You want the ultimate recipient to react favorably to you, so if your friend isn't doing that, you need to know it so you can change your letter.

When you have your final draft completed, check your spelling and punctuation to make sure it is correct. Consult a dictionary if you are not sure or use your spell checker on your computer. Do not send out poorly spelled or poorly typed letters. Ask for help from someone you know who writes well. Remember, your letter will create the first impression of you. Make it a good one.

Never hide the fact that you are looking for business projects. These executives must be informed that you are on a business marketing campaign (similar to a job hunt). But assure them that you are not going to put them in an awkward position by asking for something they might not be able or willing to give you. You are not looking for them to hire you for a project – you are merely seeking advice.

The single purpose of this introductory letter is to get you an interview where you can be seen and evaluated face-to-face.

The Thank You Letter

The most overlooked, and yet perhaps the most important, letter in this process is the thank you note which every person willing to see and talk to you should receive – no matter the outcome of the interview.

Since busy executives are willing to take valuable time to listen to you, and perhaps play an important role in actually getting you a business deal (should they want to), you should reciprocate their time and interest with common courtesy and follow up your interview with a simple thank you note.

There are also other reasons for doing this. First, one important reason is that you want to be remembered – and *remembered favorably*. Even though this specific executive may not have a business deal for you, or even a referral, such a thank you letter will help keep you remembered favorably should that time come in the future. Thank you letters are so rarely sent by interview seekers that you're bound to make a definite impression by sending one.

Secondly, if you or the executive have agreed on some follow up action, the thank you letter can *serve as a reminder* – to confirm that promised contact. If you were given advice to follow, you can mention it again in the thank you letter, thanking the executive for the idea, and stating the specific actions you are taking. This will show you listened intently and are serious about utilizing their advice.

A thank you note also provides a vehicle for *clarification*. If something was said in the interview which was confusing, misleading or cast you in a negative light, you can try to correct that impression in a thank you letter.

Write the letter the same day of the interview while it is still fresh in your memory. It would be drastic to get your interviews mixed up and write details of one meeting to the wrong executive.

Keeping Track of Your Interviews

Organization plays an important role in your interviewing. Be sure to keep accurate records, as it can quickly get confusing because there are several steps you need to take with each prospect and each interview which will progress at different rates of speed.

You may be waiting for some to receive their letters. You may be waiting to actually make contact or for call backs. You will be waiting for appointment times to arrive. You may have some appointments postponed that need to be reset. Some will be waiting for the thank you note or further follow ups.

You'll also be learning about the many advantages of loaning out your portfolios to people with a pre-arranged appointment of when you will pick it up from them. This type of "puppy dog" approach is very effective in giving you reasonable cause to come to their home. You'll be able to loan out your portfolios all the time if you seek out the opportunities and recognize them when they appear. I'll discuss this more fully later in the book. I'm telling you about this now because you'll have to have good record keeping skills to help you track all the people who have a portfolio and when you are scheduled to pick it up from them.

Referral Interview Prospect

PERSON TO CONTACT _____

POSITION _____

COMPANY_____

PHONE (   ) _____

ADDRESS _____

CITY _____ ZIP _____

EMAIL ADDRESS _____

REFERRED BY _____

REFERRAL LETTER SENT _____

FOLLOW UP CALL MADE _____

CALL BACK _____ CALL BACK _____

ASSISTANT'S NAME _____

APPOINTMENT DATE _____

TIME _____ AM PM

APPOINTMENT PLACE

_____

_____

THANK YOU NOTE SENT _____

REFERRALS RECEIVED

_____
_____
_____
_____
_____
_____
_____
_____
_____
_____
_____
_____

RESCHEDULED APPOINTMENT _____

TIME _____ AM PM   COMPLETED ☐ YES ☐ NO

This type of form is critical to have an organized system of keeping track of what stage of contact each executive is in. You can also track them in an Excel Spreadsheet, on paper or even on 4x6 index cards. You can even photo copy the form here and print off copies of it for use. Just make sure you have a system to organize all your contact and follow up information.

Always try to keep the initiative yourself but sometimes the secretary or the contact themselves will opt to call you back rather than the other way around. There will be some people who will refuse to meet with you for various reasons. Either the people will be just too busy, won't understand your wishes or just won't want to give you time. They will probably be in the minority, however.

Don't take a refusal personally. These people have pressures that put them under added time constraints so they are temporarily too busy or too worried about a personal crisis to deal with one more thing on their schedule. That's all right. Some people are over extended and it's better for you if they say "no". After all, you want your time with them to be productive – both for you and for them.

If you choose to copy and use the form printed here, after you have completed the process, check the "completed" box at the bottom of the form and file it away for possible later use. Use the back of the form to write your directions or draw a map. You can even draw a quick map. Go you can visit such websites as www.mapquest.com, enter the address of the person/company, enter your starting point and you'll be able to retrieve a map and printable written directions. Take the form with you for handy reference and put it back with your other forms when you return.

Whether you use my form or not, make sure you keep an accurate record of your contacts and progress. It's easy to get confused or to miss an important step if you don't.

Chapter Nine

Getting Past the Gatekeepers and to the Top Real Estate Agents, Home Owners or Executive Contacts

The really busy, successful real estate agents or executives are the ones you specifically want to target (when you feel ready) as they are the movers and doers. They are also very busy doing what they do best and won't be trying to stage houses or redesign their homes themselves.

Therefore, because they are so busy, getting an appointment to share your portfolio (or anything else with these people) will be difficult as a result. They will most likely have very qualified "gatekeepers", otherwise known as secretaries or administrative assistants.

It is these people's sole job when answering the phones to weed out solicitors or unimportant calls and feed only the important callers (in their opinion) to their bosses. If you don't get the gatekeeper, you might get directed to the person's voice mail in which case you either have to leave a message (and state you'll call back again or ask them to phone you) or leave no message at all and just keep trying to catch them in the office.

But most people don't realize the impact and power that secretaries and assistants have and how they can totally prevent you from ever making contact with the people you most want to connect with, so you have to build a relationship first with employees if you don't want to take months and months to get through.

So here's how to do that.

If you're lucky, you'll call the office and actually talk to a real person. If you're not so lucky, you'll have to work your way through their "automated attendant", trying to find a customer service person or receptionist. Hint: When you get an automated service, you can usually get a real person on the line by entering "0" during the process.

Once you have been connected with someone, ask them for the names of the top two agents in the company. Don't ask to be put through to them. Just get their names.

Once you have been given their names, ask for the name of their personal assistant or secretary. When you have the person's name, ask to speak to her or him.

Now here is the key. These people are just as busy as anyone else in the office and more than likely they are overworked, under-appreciated and under-paid employees. So have a great deal of respect for them and don't waste their time.

Here's what to say:

"Hi _____. My name is _____. I know you must be very busy so I will get to the point. I'm sure _____ (insert name of agent) is interested in ways to shorten the selling time on his/her listings, and I suspect may be interviewing different reps right now to accomplish this.

When do you think the best time would be to call back and ask him/her a few questions, so I can customize a proposal?"

The secretary just might say, "He's in right now, I'll put you through." or "He'll be back at 4:00, if you want to call back then."

It would be rare, or next to impossible, to get a response like, "Oh, he wouldn't be interested at all so don't bother us again." Secretaries will always appreciate someone who respects them, who acknowledges that they are busy and who is upfront, honest and direct and doesn't waste their time with phony chit chat.

They appreciate people who don't have an elitist attitude and expect others to drop everything to talk to them that instant.

And you want, more than anything, to get this secretary on your side. Think about how powerful it would be if he/she said to the agent, "Hey, you should talk to this one. She seems very professional and on top of her game."

I've been in business for a very, very long time. I've answered thousands of calls from a wide variety of people. One of the things I hate the most is to be dialed by a computer, then have to wait a few seconds for the sales person to come on the line. "Hey, I think to myself, you called me, so why do I have to wait for you to come on the line?" Whenever I hear that 3-second delay, I know right away it is a sales person and they are "dismissed" in my mind before they open their mouth. If they don't have the time to dial the phone themselves, then I'm not going to give up my time to hear their pitch.

Harsh? Well, maybe, but what they are telling me right off the bat is that their time is more important than my time. I make it a practice never to do any business with a salesperson who uses a computer to dial my number.

I also never do business with people who waste my time pretending to care about who I am or who try to pretend that I've done business with them in the past or met them somewhere before or that they are responding to some fictitious prior business deal or the like. And if someone asks me how the weather is right off the bat, or how I'm feeling or they are rude enough to neglect to introduce themselves and their company, they won't get any where with me either.

I repeat: Before you say anything, state your name and your company name. Why antagonize someone before you have even had a chance. And never, ever use a computerized message to play in your place. This is a HUGE no-no. (I just got one of those calls right now, and I hung up without listening while being irritated at the same time. Using a computer to call people is a huge mistake no matter what anyone tells you. As a consultant, it is imperative that you keep things as personable as possible. Make phone calls – don't text people or rely on email. It's not personable.)

So I believe wholeheartedly in getting to the point. I often have people who call me up, never give me their name and work overtime to hide keep from disclosing their company name. My position is this. If you have to hide who you are and who you work for, what else are you hiding?
You must do everything in your power to respect the person you are speaking with, as well as their time. Stress is everywhere and most people *feel* they are overworked even if they are not. So it's not a matter of interrupting a truly busy person as much as it is interrupting a person who *feels* overly busy and stressed. Cut them some slack.

All you're ever after on a phone call like this is to finally speak to the person you want to meet with and get an appointment. You're not going to sell anything over the phone. All you want is an appointment. And in the process, you want to be respectful, pleasant, honest and trustworthy. And if you promise to call back, be sure to call back promptly at the time you were given.

Punctuality

Punctuality is crucial at this stage of the game. Well, it's crucial at any stage, but it is even more crucial now. People have lost projects and been hired based solely on punctuality.

If a vendor makes an appointment with me, I expect his or her arrival within 5 minutes of the appointment time. Being a couple minutes early is even better. And should they be running late through no fault of their own (or especially if they goofed up), they should be sure to call me and explain the reasons for their tardiness and set a new time. NOTE: Never ever leave them hanging, wondering if you're going to show up or not. And when you state your reason, make it specific so they are less likely to think it may be just an excuse.

If someone is late and rude enough to leave me in the lurch, they don't get hired ever – not ever. Because I feel that if they treat me with disrespect on the front end, what in the world will happen to me or my project on the back end? And I think that is a reasonable concern for anyone to have.

Phoning After Your Letter Has Been Received by Your Prospect

The best referral letter in the world becomes useless if you do not follow up, phoning for an appointment. If you're shy, this may be hard for you, but you've got to do it.

The reason you haven't asked the person to phone you instead is because most won't, even if interested. And remember, I've already said to keep the initiative yourself whenever possible.

Even the best intentioned person is busy and will tend to procrastinate. So by and large, the only way to get an appointment is to call the prospect. Calling is better than email because it is more personal; but if all else fails, try emailing the person.

Here are some specific tips when phoning if you have sent a referral letter. Make sure before you phone that the person has had ample time to receive and read your letter.

Keep in mind that most people have two specific things on their mind when they receive your call: 1) Who are you? And 2) What do you want? Therefore, the first thing you MUST do is identify yourself. State your name and your company name immediately. As I've mentioned previously, I cannot tell you how many calls I get where the person does neither and it's a waste of my time and sets them up for failure with me immediately. Don't make that mistake.

Be as warm with your voice and manner as you would be in person. Put a smile on your face when speaking and the other person will pick up on your friendliness. Don't feel inferior to the other person but don't act superior either.

Let your attitude reflect expectation. Expect to speak to the person you have written. Be enthusiastic yet remain businesslike.

One of the best ways to speak confidently is to have a prepared list of the things you would like to say. It helps to write down what you wish to cover for it plants this more firmly in your mind. If the conversation shifts in a direction you hadn't anticipated, your list will also aid you in moving it back in the direction you wish to take.

Speak directly to the purpose of your call. Don't stammer or stutter. Your list will help you sound articulate. Take a few minutes and think about all the possible answers you might receive, writing down your responses. The more prepared you are to deal with the turn of the conversation, the more confidently you will speak.

This week I received a phone call from an artist. I'll call him John. He wanted to send me information, claiming to be a genius in 5 separate areas, which remained unidentified. He had not planned out what he wanted to say to me and when he did speak, he was focused on how *he* was going to benefit from sending me his portfolio. At least I think he wanted to send a portfolio. I never quite understood the purpose of his call. He got dismissed instantly as he was totally unprofessional in his attempt and clearly wasted my time.

When the Letter Has Not Been Received by the Prospect

Just because you mailed someone your letter, that doesn't mean that they got it. So one of the first things you must do is find out if the letter was received and if the prospect remembers getting it and remembers what the letter stated.

They might have received the letter but not read it yet. They might have passed it on to someone else. If they have not received it, offer to send another one. If they have not read it, ask if they would prefer you to call back the next day to give them time to read it, or hang on the phone while they read it first.

One of my students, Mary, found her first phone call unnerving. She had addressed her letter to a key executive, but when she called to speak to the person, she was told that the executive had retired three weeks previously, so Mary was connected with his replacement – something she had not anticipated.
Mary told me she found herself stammering and stuttering all because the replacement had not received her letter. What to do? She blundered through a verbal explanation of the purpose of the call, received a rather cold response (which added to her stress), and only wanted to get off the phone as soon as possible.

Upon reflection, she decided that she should have declined to talk to the replacement. She should have noted the person's name, then she should have sent them a referral letter directly, following up in a few days. *Winging it* over the phone is not a good idea unless you have plenty of phone experience of this nature and have mastered phone techniques.

Getting Past the Gate Keeper When You Have Sent a Referral Letter First

Unlike the previous technique I already wrote about, in this situation you sent a letter first and are now following up with your phone call.

One of the easiest ways to get through to the person you wish to speak to, if you aren't connected directly or don't know their 3-4 digit extension, is to say to the assistant, "Hello, I'm (your name), from (name of your company). I have already sent (name of your prospect) a letter and I'm just calling to follow up on my correspondence. May I speak to him/her?"

See how direct and easy that is?

If the assistant or receptionist asks you before you can state that, "What is this concerning?" you can simply say, "It's personal. My call is expected." No one will inquire further and will usually put you right through to the person you want to speak with.

You may be told that the person is in a meeting or just stepped out of the office or is on vacation or ill. Whatever reason you are given, try to find out when it would be a good time for you to call back. Don't "bug" the secretary with repetitive calls at times that are inconvenient for the agent or the executive. Receptionists typically know the schedules or work habits of various people in the office, so treat this person with warmth and graciousness. You've heard the saying: Treat others the way you wish to be treated.

If you've been referred by someone, particularly if that person happens to be a relative, be sure to mention this fact. If the person is not in, ask if you can go ahead and set an appointment with them. Many people overlook this possibility, but assistants are often allowed to schedule appointments. Often you will be asked if you want to be put through to the person's voice mail. Always say "yes".

When you leave your voice mail message, identify yourself by name and company name. State briefly the point of your call (to get an appointment) and state who referred you, if anyone. State that you will call back later in hopes of reaching the prospect. Leave your phone number just in case they want to call you. Consider leaving your email address as well, but do make it clear that you will follow up yourself should you not hear from them.

Never settle for an assistant's promise to have the prospect call you back. I can pretty well guarantee you that your phone will never ring. Keep the initiative yourself whenever possible. Sometimes people do call back, but it is rare.

Always come away with the secretary's name, if possible, especially if the secretary has promised to do something on your behalf. There's just something about having to give up your name to someone that makes one more responsible to actually do what is promised.

Your Prospect

Hey! The prospect is in! What next?

Remember their first concern will always be, "Who are you? What do you want?" So when you finally get your contact on the phone, be sure to identify yourself immediately.

I often have visitors to my website or students call me up and simply ask for me without identifying themselves first. I dislike this very much. I want to know who I'm talking to first and foremost. I don't think I'm alone in this type of sentiment.

Remind the person of the letter you sent previously and ask if it was received. If the answer is "yes", proceed with asking for an appointment. If the letter was not received, back off and don't press forward. It's much more effective to suggest that you send another copy of the letter and verify the address and department.

Be sure to graciously thank the person for taking time to talk to you and say you will telephone again after the second letter arrives.

If the letter has been read, state the purpose for the call – you want a brief meeting so you can ask for advice and get suggestions. You might mention again that you are not coming to ask for a business deal, nor do you expect to discuss any potential future deal. But state that based on their success in their profession, you feel they could give you some valuable direction.

Chances are you'll get your request. If the answer is "yes", mention some specific dates and times that are convenient for you. Be sure to keep an appointment book handy. Don't say you are available at any time. You don't want to appear inactive or disorganized. You can be sure, if the times you suggest are not convenient for this person, an alternative will be suggested to you.

Be sure you sound enthusiastic on the phone to meet and say you are looking forward to meeting in person. Remember, the purpose of your interview is for information only. You are not going to ask this person to do business with you. If there is any hesitancy to grant you the interview, it is most likely because the person feels you are going to put them on the spot. Clarify that you do not expect them to do anything more than share some of their expertise that might relate to your quest. One of the best ways to get hired for a pending project is to never ask to be hired.

The Outright Refusal

If you are adamantly refused by either the assistant or the prospect, don't be discouraged. There are thousands of people that will be happy to meet with you and give the guidance you seek. Simply go on to the next call. Most people are quite open and willing to help if you have taken all the pressure off, making it clear that you are not expecting anything they cannot give you freely.

Of course, there may be some who simply don't have the time to meet with you, even though they might like to do so. Don't take it as a personal affront. It's their loss, actually – you could have been the perfect solution to a problem they may now have, or may have in the future. Treat it as a helpful experience – you are closer to your next "yes".

Chapter Ten

Preparing for the Interview

If you've done the homework assignments to date you should already have a list of the initial people you will contact for your first interviews. Now you want to properly prepare yourself for those interviews.

Determine first why you want to see the person in the first place. Obviously developing a personal relationship or friendship with each one is an underlying goal. But you must have a clear picture of the overlying goal as well.

You're going to want to gather specific information from each person you meet with and that information will determine what further actions are needed. So the best way to prepare for each interview is to have a list of questions to ask. These questions might be the same for each person, but most likely will be different from one person to the next.

Getting the Interview Started

Apart from the questions you will ask, one of the most difficult parts of the process is getting started. So you'll want to prepare a brief, enthusiastic introduction to your brief meeting. Be cordial and businesslike. Immediately thank the person for taking the time to meet with you. These are very busy people; be appreciative of their willingness to help you in any way.

Reassure the person that you're not trying to strike a business deal with them of any kind. Reassure them that you don't even expect them to know of one. It's important to re-emphasize this because letters are usually scanned and these points might have been missed.

Just because your letter was received, that doesn't mean it was read thoroughly. It also doesn't mean that it was fully understood nor remembered. In the time lapse between the receipt of the letter, the phone call making the appointment and the actual interview, the pertinent facts of your letter most likely have been forgotten and you need to rehearse these at the start of any meeting.

Don't forget – one of the most important items is to *restate verbally that you are not there to do a business deal.* It's better to reinforce this issue once again than to have the meeting start out "cold" and remain that way when it is so easy to avoid.

Next you'll want to state the purpose of your meeting. In a job interview, a candidate should always include a Mission Statement or Objective at the beginning of their resume. You must have one as well.

Early in the meeting you will want to hand your portfolio to the person to preview. But while they are reading your portfolio, you don't want to sit there staring at them. That will make them feel uncomfortable. So pull out some literature or busy yourself with doing something quietly so that the person doesn't feel compelled to skim your material in a hurry. You want them to feel comfortable enough to take as much time as they need to go through your portfolio from start to finish.

After they have finished, you're ready to talk to them. A logical place to start would be to say, "Thank you so much for looking over my portfolio. Based on my mission statement (or stated objective), do you think my portfolio tells a compelling story? Does it support my objective?"

As you can see, a question of this nature gets you immediately into the mindset of asking for their advice and you should find what happens next a mind-opening, hopefully positive experience.

You can easily refer to any section of your portfolio to make whatever points you wish to stress. Ask the person to give you an overall evaluation of the portfolio and ask if it makes sense to them.

When you have done this, go to your prepared list of questions. Feel free to take a list of questions with you and refer to them if it makes you feel more comfortable. As you get accustomed to interviewing prospects and contacts, you will develop confidence and have less need for notes.

Give your prospect or contact time to think and respond to your questions. Always listen attentively. Don't put your head down; this is not attentive listening. You need eye contact and you must visually respond or they will think you're not listening. Nod your head in agreement. Ask follow-up questions to comments they make. Take notes.

When you need clarification, ask for it. These are all ways they will know you are listening and that you feel they are giving you valuable information.
Wait until the end of the meeting to ask for suggestions of one or two people you could talk to next to get additional information and advice. You must first establish *rapport* with the current prospect before they will be willing to lend you their "good name" to continue your interviewing process.

In addition to this, they have to have a good idea of *where* you want to go before they can intelligently suggest someone else with whom you could talk.

Ask for referrals in the specific area you are interested in – whether staging or redesign. You'll probably begin your process with professionals or homeowners in fields totally separate from yours. If they cannot think of anyone at the moment, offer to call in a few days so they have time to think about it and gather the contact information for you.

Set a date to call back. Be sure the prospect knows you will *not* be asking these people for a business deal either. Don't assume they will know that; make sure they do.

Tell them you will be on an active campaign and would appreciate being kept in mind in case they hear of anything in the future. Then thank them again for their time and say you will keep them informed of your progress. You have now left the door open to being considered favorably in the future in the event they want to hire you for a project or hear of something they think you might be interested in.

Questions You Can Ask Your Prospect

Here is a list of sample questions you could ask when meeting with your prospects and contacts. Pick out the ones that fit the situation and the person you will be meeting with. Write down others that apply to each specific meeting you conduct.

1. Is my stated objective or mission statement supported by my portfolio materials?
2. Have I sufficiently highlighted my experience and skills through my portfolio?
3. Are my skills and accomplishments specific enough or too general?
4. Considering my background, do you feel I will be effective?

5. Hypothetically, in solving the problems of home owners and real estate agents, where do you see my background being most helpful?
6. Have you any advice for improving my overall presentation?
7. Are there any individuals you would suggest I contact that could guide me further?
8. If you were conducting a meeting such as this, what specific types of people, contacts or organizations would you seek advice from?
9. What future do you visualize for my industry?
10. To broaden my perspective, is there anyone in your firm or organization you would recommend that I contact?
11. What materials or books, if any, might I read to increase my knowledge for building a business such as this?
12. What are some of the most important things you would look for if you were considering contracting someone with my background and mission statement?
13. Do you mind if I use your name as a referral when I contact _____?
14. May I keep you posted on my progress?

Length of Time

The ideal length of time for a meeting of this type is anywhere from 15 minutes to one hour. Most interviews of this nature take about 40-45 minutes. Bear in mind that some of the most productive interviews have been as short as 15-20 minutes, so length does not determine quality. There are people who love to talk and can go on for two hours; if they want to, let them. Good listeners get the reputation of being *very* intelligent and professional.

If time is brief, consider leaving your portfolio behind and invite the prospect to read it over at his or her leisure. They will probably give it a more thorough read and will appreciate the pressure-less ability to absorb the material without you being present. This is also great for you because it gives you the perfect reason for returning at another time to discuss it later when they have more time.

Never try to accomplish anything with your prospect if you sense they are distracted or pressed for time. You don't have to weaken your case by having to fight for their attention. It's too important. Yes, it's more work for you to come back. But going to the effort to return later is well worth it if it means getting hired or not.

Should your prospect want or need to discuss anything with their spouse in your absence, they have your thoroughly prepared portfolio to take home so that the spouse is equally impressed with you and your expertise. Sending home a portfolio is far more powerful than a mere business card or brochure. Try to arrange it pick it up again at their home because, after all, this is the place where you want to work.

Obstacles

When someone suggests an obstacle to your path, ask for advice on how you can overcome it. Cooperate with them in finding a solution. Perhaps you'll end up making an alteration in your final objective because of insurmountable problems you hadn't anticipated.

If your prospect or contact cannot suggest a resolution to a problem, ask for a referral to someone they think could. You see, there is no end to the amount of help you could get as you journey through the process of getting your business to grow.

Chapter Eleven

The
Referral Interview

For some people, the idea of "making referral interviews" is threatening and they don't want to step out the front door. Believe me, I've been there myself. But you know the saying, "No pain – no gain." You've got to push yourself through the fear by concentrating on your message and how you're going to be able to help people once they know about you. When your focus is on you, fear increases; when your focus is *not* on you, fear diminishes.

This process is fun. You should discover that the interviews are enjoyable and highly profitable, particularly if you've made a pre-decision to enjoy yourself and everyone you meet. They are opportunities for you to meet successful people who are usually not only interesting but can be funny and extremely helpful. There is no reason to be fearful of this process.

You will be meeting with fellow human beings who, for the most part, will be pretty fair-minded individuals willing to help you if they can. They generally want to say "yes" and they dislike having to reject anyone. You won't be asking for anything they cannot give you. And since most people enjoy receiving recognition for their own accomplishments, they will feel flattered that you have sought them out for advice.

There is something else. People prefer to be approached gradually. They do not like being surprised nor pressured into anything. I, for one, will leave a retail store immediately if a sales clerk starts to follow me around or starts to pressure me into looking at something they suggest. I want to be left alone when shopping to look at my leisure without any pressure. When I'm ready to buy something, I will take it to the checkout counter myself.

I'm not alone in this sentiment. I think you'll find that people feel the same way in their office or home. Pressure tactics almost never work any more and usually business deals done in this manner tend to unwind quickly once the sales person has gone away.

If you were to enter their office or home asking immediately for a business deal, the whole process will be short-circuited because you will make the prospect feel uncomfortable from the start. (Obviously this does not apply when a desire to enter into a business deal has already been decided and communicated.)

The whole reason for a referral interview is to enter into a meaningful discussion with someone else about your portfolio and its effectiveness in communicating your message. That is all the meeting is intended to accomplish. It is an excellent way to gain information. It is also an excellent way to make contacts that could eventually lead to business deals.

Why You Should Never Ask for a Business Deal in a Referral Interview

The reason you should never ask to do business with the prospect is that it is unlikely that person will have a need for your service at that exact moment. If you ask to do business that day, you instantly put them in a position of having to say "no". This makes them uncomfortable. When they feel uncomfortable, they begin wishing you'd leave.

Very few "cold" requests get deals. On the other hand, it is not inconceivable that an interview moves gradually and naturally from an interview for feedback into a business deal. But that process happens as a result of the sharing of information back and forth. It usually is spawned by the prospect and not by you.

By the same token, never *hide* the fact that you are looking for multiple business deals. It is imperative that the prospect or contact know that you are on an active marketing campaign to connect with people who have a need for your service.

You are not, however, expecting them to be the one to give it to you. You want them to remember you favorably. If they feel no pressure from you they will listen more intently, feel free to make suggestions to you and then remember you in a positive light once you are gone.

Needs arise at a later time and if you are remembered, you may be invited back for another interview. Second interviews usually wind up in business deals.

Purpose of the Referral Interview

There are several benefits and reasons for making referral interviews. The first objective is to *establish rapport with your prospect*, building some kind of mutually beneficial relationship. The best way to do that is to show a genuine interest in your prospect. Most people going to an interview concentrate solely on themselves and their need to land a deal, talking as much about themselves as possible in the belief that they will get a contract if the prospect sees their qualities. However, prospects are equally interested in impressing you with their fine qualities, so if you do all the talking, you probably will not be remembered very favorably.

Get to know the prospect or contact. Be certain they know and understand your objective, but get to know them as well. See them as individuals involved in their own quest for success. Get them to talk. This is not only an effective way to build a strong rapport with them, but it also gives you valuable inside information from an outsider's perspective that can be very useful to you.

I often get calls from visitors to my website who want additional information about my courses, books and products, but instead of asking questions to get the information they seek, they spend an exorbitant amount of time trying to impress me with statements like, "My friends are always asking me to come over to help them", after which they launch into one example after another. This is ok, but doesn't do much to get them remembered favorably because the claims are all so generic and commonly espoused. It's as if they feel some compelling need to convince me of something about them. If it were necessary, it would be much better done in person with a portfolio and not over the phone.

The second objective is *to give and receive information.* Your contact is someone who can advise you – not someone who can "pull strings for you". If you leave with more information than you arrived with, it has been a successful interview. Knowledge is power and the more you have, the easier it is to build your business.

Your third objective is to *get advice on your personal marketing campaign.* Your prospect will react to you in a certain way. Your goal is to discover that reaction and why it happened. There aren't that many experts around when it comes to evaluating a portfolio, so the comments and suggestions from these *professionals* can really improve your effectiveness. Your prospect will be *totally* objective in evaluating you, your presentation and your business goals. And they will be pleased that you value their opinions.

Referral interviews are really means of *building a network of contacts*. One person will refer you to someone else, who may refer you to two or three others, each of whom may refer you to at least one other person.

Where you started with one contact, now you have at least 8 – perhaps more or less – but certainly more than the one you started with. Therefore, if an interview has not turned from an interview into a business deal, you will be asking for (and probably receiving) referrals to others from whom a business deal could develop.

Your prospect will probably be happy to refer you to other people because you have already demonstrated that you will not be asking them for anything other than advice and information as well.

When you ask someone to look at your portfolio and your mission statement (or objectives), make suggestions and give you advice, you make them a "partner" in your campaign. They automatically want to see you get what you want. They now have a small stake in your future. They have given you some of their valuable time and would like to see it pay off.

If no referrals are offered, they may be considering you for a business deal now or in the near future. In any event, no matter the outcome, you should come away with useful information that will improve your business right away. Each interview you finish will increase your professionalism and your confidence.

Finally, do not overlook the importance of being *remembered favorably and actively.* You do not want to end the interview with a mere thank you and best wishes for a successful future. You want to keep the relationship open by asking for permission to keep them informed of your progress.

As your "partner", they usually will be glad to hear from you again. This also keeps your name current in their mind in the event circumstances change and they decide they want to do business with you. For that reason, I stress writing everyone a thank you note within 24 hours of your interview – even the secretary or assistant who put your call through to your prospect.

I have established myself more favorably in people's minds by going the extra mile with a thank you. Don't rely on phone calls or email here. Make it a personal note card or letter – something that shows you went to extra time and effort to send to them. It's not just simple courtesy – it's good business.

Therefore, as you progress in building your business, be sure to follow-up and keep in touch with past prospects and contacts to let them know of your progress. Let them know when a business deal has been transacted and a few of the details. Relate your story in an interesting manner. By doing so, you will maximize all of your contacts to the fullest and brilliantly extend your possibilities.

Your Attitude

Keep a positive and affirmative attitude. Do *not* under any circumstances go *to an interview if you are pre-occupied, troubled or depressed.* If necessary, call up and postpone the appointment, but don't try to "cover up" your problem. It will show through and only do you more harm than good. There is enough stress automatically built into the process of marketing your business without adding more.
If an interview has been granted, you should have no difficulty getting a postponement, providing you do not keep postponing it.

Always keep control of your process. This is why you want to do all the follow-up work yourself. Keep the initiative. After all, no one cares as much about building your business as you do. Don't depend on someone else to do your leg-work for you, because that usually guarantees you'll go no where soon.

Do not under market yourself. Don't settle for less than you know you are capable of doing and being. You only hurt yourself. Look for ways that will constantly challenge you to the best life has to offer. Hold your head high, no matter what your past. Remember, you are marketing your future.

Never ask for a business deal. If the opportunity presents itself naturally, it should come from your prospect based on a careful evaluation of you, your portfolio and the exchange of ideas. When done correctly, a business deal should be forthcoming if there is a present need for your services.

Use questions. The best way to get information is to ask questions. Questions are a guaranteed way to open up a meaningful dialog on any topic of choice. Plan your questions in advance. Have a list handy. Questions are also the most effective way you have to keep the prospect talking.

When the referral interview ends, *keep it open* by asking for permission to report back. Always ask the prospect what they feel is your **next** step – not what is their next step. Here again, keep the initiative. You are the one taking action – not your prospect.

Eventually You Have to Ask for the Business

Eventually you must ask for the business you want. But it needs to be done only after you have built a relationship with your prospects. Then it will come naturally and most likely will be received with warmth.

Chapter Twelve

Dress Codes for Interviews

Your appearance is part of you and has a strong influence on your prospect. Therefore you want to be neat and clean. It shouldn't need to be stated, but it is. Do not wear clothes or a hairstyle that so dominate and attract self attention that *you* are lost in the shuffle. Dress in basic business attire.

John T. Malloy wrote two excellent books on the subject of business attire: *The Woman's Dress for Success Book* and *Dress for Success* (for men). He suggests men wear suits and women should wear a skirted suit or a dress with coordinating jacket. Styles here in California are very relaxed now, but it's better to be slightly overdressed than to be underdressed.

It's good to have several business outfits as you may very likely be going back to meet with some of your contacts additional times and you don't want to wear the same outfit. The more successful the person is you are meeting with, the more likely you will have a *series* of meetings with the same person before any business deal is consummated.

Interestingly enough, the best colors for success are reported to be gray, blue, brown and beige. It is important to dress in a manner that you can maintain throughout your business and in keeping with the average consultant in our industry.

You can always feel safe in a conservative outfit. To save money, do "cross shopping". This means you buy clothing of a look, quality and feel similar to the more expensive upper-middle class brands but purchase it at discount stores or on the web where prices may be considerably less expensive.

Don't wear excessive jewelry. You do not want to appear more financially successful than your contact or prospect. Wear subdued scents or no scent at all. Wear brown shoes with brown apparel and black with black apparel. Have your shoes clean and polished. Do not wear low cut tops or chipped fingernail polish, ladies. I shouldn't have to include this, but unfortunately I feel I must.

When it comes to doing business with someone, you will increase your chances if you:

- Dress well (no jeans, and ladies, wear bra)
- Have clean fingernails
- Use business English
- Don't fiddle with objects on desk
- Wear a suit rather than sport coat
- Wear shorter, neatly trimmed hair
- Men, have clean shaven face
- Wear clean, pressed, conservative apparel
- Use mouth wash and deodorant
- Don't chew gum

I know of two people specifically who were hired based on their "look" rather than their experience or talent.

Arrive early enough to visit the restroom. Make last minute touch up to hair, clothing, breath and overall appearance.

To sum up, dress for the occasion. Give yourself and your prospect the respect due to you both. Dress well. It's important. Turn off your cell phone or put it on vibrate.

Nerves – How to Control Them

Eat a cracker to settle stomach acids if your stomach feels queasy. It probably will only happen on the first interview you do. After that you'll see how easy they are and should relax more.

Never drink alcohol before an interview. It will dull your senses and reactions, decrease your mental faculties and generate a noticeable aroma that will not be appreciated. Never take any tranquilizing drugs either. Stimulants may make you hyper and fidgety. Avoid artificial stimuli.

Just be yourself – that's the best way to conduct business. Your future and happiness can be affected positively or negatively because of this interview, but no matter the outcome, it can never be disastrous to your future. There are millions of people out there waiting to be contacted. Each interview is just one person in the whole scheme of things.

After the interview ends, go treat yourself! You deserve a reward for taking another step to build your future.

Chapter Thirteen

Face Language

The science of "personology" has been around for a long time. It is the science of studying facial traits which are believed to give clues as to one's personality characteristics. It's quite fascinating, actually.

Studies have shown that physical traits which become very prominent in a person's face are indicative of a personality trait. Someone once said, "Before 30, God is responsible for your face, but after 30, *you* are responsible for it."

The older a person is, the more pronounced certain traits are likely to be, so an understanding of some of them might help you key into the personality of your prospect or contact the moment you meet.

Here are a few of the traits I find quite interesting and more common. When you look at a person's face, focus only on the traits that jump out at you and are more noticeable. But bear in mind this is not an exact science. It's included here for what value it might bring you, but nothing is "written in stone".

Make your mental notations when you first sit down to talk. This should give you some guidance on what type of person you will spend the next few minutes with and how better to relate to them.

Later you can re-evaluate to see if your first impressions were accurate or not. It's a fun way to do an interview and add an extra element of secret fun to the process.

Full, Loose Lips
Generosity. Glad to stay late, work Saturdays, help in emergencies. Tend to take time and might ramble. Generous about gifts.

Tight, Thin Lips
Concise. Prefers that people be brief and to the point. Tendency to be curt.

Upturned Lips
Optimism. Inclined to figure things will work out well. Usually pleasant and pleasing to be with.

Down-turned Lips
Pessimism. Anticipates unhappy outcomes. Less fun to be with.

Large Irises
Emotionality. Affectionate. Takes everything to mean whether you like them or not. Warm personality.

Small Irises
Hidden Emotionality. Matter-of-fact nature. Does not show sentiment easily.

White Under Iris
Gloominess, Melancholy. May have heavy problems or unhappy situation. Expect little enthusiasm. Will tend to unload woes if given a chance.

Slanted Eyes (down on outside corner)
Criticalness/Critical Perception. Good adviser. Will notice your flaws. Generally not complimentary.

Slanted Eyes (up on outside corner)
Lack of Criticalness. Not likely to be nagger nor incisive. Enjoyable to be with. May handle situations poorly for failing to see disadvantages as well as advantages.

Luminous, Sparkling Eyes
High Magnetism. Alert nature, interested in life. Joy to be with. Attract people around them.

Glassy Eyes
Under Pressure. Under strain/borrowing energy. Be careful around this person until more relaxed or under control.

Upper Eyelid Hidden
Analytical. Always figuring things out. Must know why and where before making decisions. May seem stubborn. Needs to hear reasons and validations.

Upper Eyelids Visible
Minimal Analytical. Direct actionist who will jump in and do things. Impulsive. Can cut through situations and get things done. May not stop to think how others feels.

Wide Set Eyes
High Tolerance. More easygoing, less concerned about rules and regulations. Willing to let others live their own lives. Easy to be around. May let people take advantage of their easy nature.

Close Set Eyes
Low Tolerance. Very concerned people. Want things the way they should be. Want performance, not good intentions. Worry about how others do.

Worry Lines Between Eyebrows
Exactingness. Tend to be fussy. Be sure you are on time. Tend to double check things, worry about past deeds.

Lines From Outside Corner of Eyes
Humor. Lots of laugh lines. Can be kidded. Enjoyable to be with.

Lines From Edge of Nose to Edge of Mouth
Oral Self-expression. Often prominent in attorneys, teachers, salespeople or other who express themselves routinely with meaning. Speak decisively. Will mean what they say.

Lines From Inner Corner Eye, Fanning Outward, Down the Cheekbone
Rhetorical. Are pleased by the right word or a brilliant flow of words. Will be precise in verbage. Excellent vocabulary. Probably good with languages.

Roman or Hawk Nose
Commercial-minded. Naturally more administrative. Like to talk business and prices. May seem impersonal or businesslike, even in intimate situations.

Concave Nose
Administrative. Spontaneously helpful. May have little interest or knack in business or money matters. Love to help. Active in religious or non-profit organizations.

High Arched Eyebrows
Dramatic. Have dramatic touches which bring things to life. Creative. Live and move with a flare. Tend to be motivated by performing, especially before groups.

Flat Eyebrows
Esthetic. Usually interested in some form of art, music, literature. Seeks beauty and harmony. Make an art out of living. Are upset by discord or disorder.

High Eyebrows

Discriminate. Like privacy. Very selective in making friends. Like things to be done in good taste. Will take time before extending friendship, but once accepting will give total friendship. May appear stuck-up and distant.

Eyebrows Close to Eyes

Affableness. Friendly and approachable. Make friends easily. Tend to be informal.

Pair of Developed Protuberances Above Eyebrows

Detail Concern. Can rise to big occasions, but tend to be upset by trifles. Do not like detail. Likes social events.

Ledge Across Lower Forehead

Methodical. Have their own system. You will make points if you fit in with it. Must tell them your desires early enough so they can work into their plans. Tend to form habits. Plan ahead.

Coarser Hair and Skin

High Texture. Usually have more rugged builds. Are more durable and can "take it". Enjoy outdoors. More basic and primal. Speak plainly. Hints or subtleties will not register.

Baby Fine Hair, Delicate Skin

Fine Texture. Generally more sensitive physically. Gravitate to refinement. Have expensive tastes. Emphasize quality, not quantity.

Round Face With Curved Forehead

Conservative. Usually jolly, jovial. The borne host and politician. Love food. Like to be asked to dinner. Distressed by seeing anything thrown out or going to waste.

Square, Angular Forehead

Construction. The career person – the builder. Need to be involved in accomplishing something tangible. Not interested in maintaining or conserving.

Stone-like Firmness of Face and Flesh

Hard. Mean what they say. Hard to make impression on them, physically or mentally. Poker faced. Do not share personality. Do not smile easily or give much feedback.

Saggy Flesh Under Chin

Soft. Respond easily but have trouble carrying through. Need direction.

Thin Face

Low Ego. Needs to be complimented.

Special Notes

- To please your prospect, adapt to his/her traits, if possible
- Your smile is more important than your words.
- Use trait indicators as a clue to start conversation
- Discover your own facial traits
- Work to minimize traits that work against you
- Confirm your trait analysis after the interview and do 3 things for your prospect or contact that fit in with their traits and that you know they would appreciate.

Remember: It's always the extreme trait which makes the individual. Skip trait indications which are medium and direct full attention on the ones that are pronounced.

Chapter Fourteen

Tips for Photos
and More

It's important to include a photograph of yourself in your materials. But what usually annoys me is when someone plasters their photograph just about everywhere.

One popular item that sales people have left at my door is a small notepad. You know the kind, I'm sure. But I have never want to use the notepads because of the overly blatant advertising and the person's photo is too prominently displayed on every page.

So if you're creating any materials to leave with a prospect or client or to be dropped off in a neighborhood, keep your advertising and especially your photo small and in a discrete place or it may just get thrown out.

It's not necessary to pay a professional photographer to shoot your picture. A head shot is all you need. If you're doing it yourself, make sure the background behind you is not distracting or overly busy.
The photo could be taken of you at your desk, sitting at a table, sitting in your living room, standing in front of a home. The background is not very important. But whatever you do, it should not draw attention away from you.

If you have blond hair, choose a background that is dark so that your hair will contrast with the background. If you have dark hair, choose a light background so you get contrast in reverse.

I always recommend you shoot against a plain background, more like a studio shot, but many people like a more casual look. I happen to like both as you'll see below. I chose to sit in front of some dark plants.

Standing beside a real estate "sold" sign can be helpful, but it also may suggest to people that you are a real estate agent. And unless you are, you don't want to send that message.

If you have an outdoor sign for your business, with your company name on the sign, you could stand beside it.

Get a friend or family member to take your picture. It's important to smile and look relaxed and friendly. Stern faces never work.

Choose an angular shot, not a full face shot. Angular shots create a better feeling of depth and you can literally choose which angle works best for you.

I have a slight scar on the left side of my face (don't bother looking for it), so photographs of me are best taken with my right side facing the camera.

Or perhaps you're having a bad hair day and your hair looks better from one angle than the other. Of course, if you're having a bad hair day, maybe you should wait for a good hair day. It's important to have your picture taken when you're feeling good about your looks.

Like it or not, people will judge you by your looks. Some people will determine totally whether they want to hire you or not based on your looks, so it is incumbent to look as nice and professional as possible. It shouldn't be like that, but let's face reality. It is.

Study your face in a mirror and look at different angles. Use a digital camera because you want to see your photos instantly so you can continue to shoot pictures if you don't find any that are usable. You will also want photos that will reproduce well on the internet as well as in your literature.

Have pictures taken with the camera even with your face. Take other pictures from slightly above and slightly below your face.

When the camera is slightly below your face, your cheekbones will be accentuated and give you more definition. This might enhance your beauty.

Don't hide behind your hair. It is important that people see your eyes. You can tell a lot about a person from their eyes, which is why there is a famous saying, "The eyes are the window of the soul."

Your eyes should be friendly, but be careful not to squint.

I recently saw a lady being interviewed on TV by a popular talk show host. She was smiling fully, but in the process her eyes literally disappeared into her face and the viewer could only see slits where her eyes had been before. You don't want this.

Some comments must have been made to her about this, I think, because several months later I saw her being interviewed again and she was careful not to smile so much. This time we could actually see her eyes.

Since I want my picture to reflect my level of expertise too, I usually wear black for photos. Black clothing suggests authority and you want to convey the feeling of authority in a subliminal way as well as in your conduct and speech.

Cameras to Consider

I own two different digital cameras as well as a conventional camera (one has a wide angle lens and one does not). I must tell you up front that I know little to nothing about cameras, so what I write here is certainly not any kind of expert guidance, but I'll share what works for me. I'm going to include some data I've gleaned from others in the field as well as my own experience, but for the best advice, please discuss your needs with a photographer at a local camera store. Equipment changes so quickly and new and improved models are always coming on the market, so for the latest and best advice, it's good to talk to the professionals.

My wide angle digital camera is an Olympus C-7070, which I like very, very much. It has been dependable and takes very good pictures, inside and outside. I bought it because, at the time, it was one of the only digital cameras available with a wide angle lens built in. It was rather pricey as I recall, being somewhere in the $700 range.

You will find out very quickly how important it is to have a wide angle lens no matter what type of camera you are using.

My second digital camera is a Panasonic Lumix DMC-FZ5 which I use for close ups because it has a 12X Optical Zoom. I must admit I'm not very good with this one and it is difficult to get it to focus properly, especially if you're standing close to the object you want to photograph. It was less expensive, somewhere in the $350 range, when purchased. I rely on it far less than I do the wide angle Olympus when in the field.

Five Tips From Other Stagers and Redesigners

Tip One - "I feel right at home answering this question. I have been a professional photographer since 1980. I feel that if I could give only one answer I would tell you to use additional sources of light when taking indoor photographs. But since I can give more advice I will! It is best to stand in the same spot and in the same stance while taking before and after pictures, to make sure you are in the same spot put an "X" on the floor with masking or painters tape and hold your camera up to your focusing eye and lock your elbows vertical to your ribcage. Take more than one or two pictures, I personally like to take panoramic shots all around the room, making sure to include the ceiling and the flooring. Remember, if shooting head on into a window or mirror you could get what is called a flare or reflection of light from the flash in your photographs (these are not ghostly spirits) and will distract from your finished work. Don't over look putting your name and logo on the pictures being used for more advertising and promotion."

Tip Two - "To add extra lighting 1. Turn on all of the lights in the room that you are photographing as well as any adjoining rooms so that the light can flood in. 2. I like to use "up lighting" in the corners of the room. I have little can lights that I purchased from a home improvement store. These lights will not sync with a flash but add a good amount of extra light. Unless you are an artist flares are hard to remove. The best thing to do is to avoid making a flare. This is why I take more than a couple of shots. To try to avoid flares 1. Do not shoot directly into a reflective object. 2. If there is no way to shoot around the object take multiple shots using variable positions such as standing on a step stool and slightly shooting down and off to either side of the object, in a standing position, put the object off to the far left or right side of the frame of your picture, or in a crouching position, shoot up and off to either side of the object. Having a digital camera helps because you can see instantly what you have just taken."

Tip Three - "Years ago I was doing seasonal color analysis for makeup and clothing. So many people had terrible home lighting that I bought a folding tripod reflector light and a full spectrum photographic light bulb. It probably cost me $80 but 15 yrs later I am still using that same bulb and stand. It is invaluable for lighting rooms or vignettes for photographic purposes. It is what I always reach for when deep cleaning or painting a room because of the superior wide angle illumination. Even in an empty white room it helps me see areas where the paint to thin while painting. It has also been great for hanging new light fixtures and examining dark spaces of all kinds like basements and attics. Keep a heavy duty extension cord with it."

Tip Four - "After seeing some comparison photos I realize that it is a necessity to have a wide angle lens for your digital camera especially when taking room photos. *I hear the GROANS, more money!* Since you are staging, likely for someone who is selling, flattering photos become extremely important and your client likely will need excellent photos for an agent and internet presentation. The other key to good photography is good lighting and you may want to invest in a small fold up photo reflector and up-lights to maximize textured surfaces or create special effects around plants, stairwells, etc. Of course, you will charge your customer for these photographs since you invested time and have expenses to cover for a disc, special lens, lighting, etc and taking photos for others use is not part of staging but a specialty service of its own. If your photos are more flattering to the clients home than those taken by the realty company, whose do you think they will want posted on the internet, TV, handouts or brochures?"

Tip Five - "Recently done extensive research into which camera would be best (and reasonably affordable) for DIY professional looking interior photographs. Found only specific reviews for óutdoor use, but by reading, reading, reading + deciding little by little what I wanted from the camera, I found Nikon, Canon and Pentax Digital SLRs to be best suitable.

In combination with a 10 - 20 mm. wide-angle lens (or 10-17/ 12 -20 depending on brand). Found out: as for quality of the photo's (right colors/ sharpness/ contrast/ depth), the lens is of só much more importance than the camera-body!

These 10 - 20 mm. lenses reach from moderately wide-angle to very wide-angle, which by the way show a lot less disfigurement of the image (rounded lines) than the classic fisheye-lenses. And don't we want to create incrédibly spacy-looking rooms?

Those lenses cost as much as the camera body, but are very light-sensitive (important for indoor use!) and produce much better quality pictures compared to those made with the 18 - 55 mm. kit-lenses (= moderately wide-angle till a bit tele, comparable to the analogous SLR 27 - 82,5 mm).

But because the 18-55 mm. lens might come in handy for 'normal' pictures, I myself decided to go for the Pentax K200D + 18-55 (just waiting a little bit longer, prices are steadily going down right now), because (= the criteria I figured out to be important for our business):

-   Pentax has the best quality kit-lens (all glass instead of the plastic Nikon + Canon). And the most affordable 10 - 17 lens (or Sigma 10 - 20).

And the body:
- is weatherproof (for the curb appeal, sometimes it just doesn't stop raining...),
- has shake-reduction (handy for indoor use: low light + slow timing (?)),
- dust-removal (véry important if you switch lenses now and then),
- is light as for weight, but steady enough (standing in the wind, or while bending over in an awkward position),
- uses standard AA-batteries (available really everywhere in case you run out of energy)
- and (seems to be) very user-friendly (...but maybe I'll buy the Pentax K10D instead which enables to regulate more features manually).

Nikons + Canons with comparable features are a lot more expensive (at least here in the Netherlands, might be different in the US?).

Interesting URL which shows well the full reach of 10-20 lenses (and the different pictures different brand lenses produce): http://www.pbase.com/alinla/1017_vs_1020"

My thanks go out to the many contributors in my forum. But again it's best to do your own research to find what is best for you and your budget.

Converting Photographs

When you are preparing photographs for the internet or for printed materials, the image must be digital or converted from a "continuous tone" (photograph) to a "half-tone" (image comprised of small dots). Half tones are kind of old school as nowadays most people use digital cameras.

But there are different file formats and types of compression to be considered. If you're using the image on the internet, you want to compress it so you'll get a fast download on the page. No sense in having your photo on a page that is so large it takes forever to display, causing your visitor to leave before they ever see it.

So in most cases, the images you'll use on your website should be JPEG format. GIF formats are degraded images from the get-go and should probably be avoided, as well as bit mat images (bmp), which are good for line drawings but not for photos.

Microsoft Word, at least as far as I know, only gives you the ability to insert a JPEG format into a document you prepare in that program. Since most people have Word on their computers, it is a good format and can also be used on the internet.

But a JPEG image will probably not be good enough for your printed materials though many online companies that will print projects for you require your images be in JPEG (jpg) format.

The standard resolution for images for best quality on a printed project is 300 ppi (pixels per inch). If you're using a line drawing, use 600 ppi.

If you have a graphics software program that allows you to edit your images, this can be very handy. I use Paint Shop Pro but most people recommend Adobe Photoshop Elements. There is a professional version available, but you don't need it. The Elements program has fewer features than the Pro version but it still offers all of the legendary quality of the Pro version.

You might also consider buying a basic book on photo editing, but don't do that unless you're planning on using a whole lot of photos in your marketing materials. It's always good to know, however, no matter what you're doing.

Use the simplest color mode available. If you're having something printed in black and white (such as I'm doing in this book), your image should be saved in "grayscale". Otherwise you'll want everything in color, I'm sure.

Manipulating Photos

There are going to be times when a client insists on you leaving some piece of furniture or accessory in its place for some reason. You'd love to move it elsewhere or remove it altogether, but you can't. And because of that, your "after" photo is going to be ruined. Don't be unduly alarmed.

If you have a client who wants you to keep something in a place that just doesn't look right, or the room stumped you and you couldn't really get the room rearranged where you were totally satisfied, you have two choices.

1) Move the furniture where you really want it and shoot your "after" shot – then move the furniture where the client insists you put it.

2) See if you can manipulate the picture later and move the item to a better place or remove it from the picture altogether.

That's the beauty of digital images. Can't always be done, but many times you can manipulate a photo for your purposes at a later time. Then you'll have a more useable picture. It's better to alter your image afterwards than to show a picture where things don't look right and you feel you have to explain why to the next prospect or client.

I have had to do this a few times myself (remove smudges, remove cords, remove paint testing samples, lower a picture, take out nicks from furniture, crop in, remove your reflection in a mirror, and so forth).

I've had a client or their child or my partner inadvertently get into a shot and I didn't know it until afterwards, strange as that may seem. I once had a client's child, hiding behind a chair, pop up his head just as I clicked the picture and I didn't notice him until later when I got back to my office.

Most digital image software comes with tools that allow you to go back in and change colors, add and remove, crop, lighten or darken and a myriad of other clever options. If you're creative, you can sometimes fix a picture for later use, which is better than going back to the home later to get the shot again. You can never get a "before" shot again, but if all else fails, and you don't have any usable shots of a room afterwards, I think it is worth returning to the home to capture some if you can.

This example was done with Paint Shop Pro but most people prefer Adobe Photoshop and I'm sure there are many more that will do an excellent job for you. You can save money by purchasing an older version which will do just fine. Here's an example of a manipulated before and after picture. Notice the imbalance of pictures to the right and left of the window.

To help show the importance of balance, more artwork was added mechanically to the shot below. The picture was also lightened. One of the problems I see most often is that candid shots come out too dark. The need to lighten them up is a pretty common adjustment you

might face, depending on your knowledge and skill working with your camera. Using a digital camera is far preferable to a film camera. One can always scan developed pictures, but it's just a whole lot easier to work with a good, dependable digital camera.

Depending on the size of reproduction and the quality of the image and your ability to manipulate, you can see how you can do some corrective work to improve your "after" picture in certain circumstances. Not that this is something that comes up often – because it doesn't. I just throw it in here to show you that all is not lost if you find out too late that your after shots are not very usable and you can't go back to the space to re-shoot them.

As previously stated, I use an Olympus C-7070 Wide Zoom digital camera for my wide angle shots. I use a Panasonic Lumix with 12X optical zoom for tight close-ups. I'm not recommending these – just saying these cameras were excellent choices at the time I purchased them. They might not be available at press time and there are conceivably better choices available for you so please seek expert advice before making your final selection.

Chapter Fifteen

How to Shoot the Best, Most Attractive Photos

Here are some do's and don'ts tips that will help you feature the best assets of the home you're staging and avoid the pitfalls that many stagers make when shooting the outside and inside of the home.

Remember, that depending on the usage of the picture, you may only have a very small display window. For instance, if the image is to be displayed on the internet, whether on your website or another one, images must be compressed for fast downloads, so only a small postage stamp size might be available or something just slightly bigger.

So it is incumbent upon you to take several shots of the home, both outside and inside when the work is done, so that you can choose the best shot available for the method you will use to market the home or your staging or redesign services.

The smaller the display area, the more difficult it is to get a really useful shot. So the tighter you get, the more contrast you have. The more illumination you have the better.

Following are some random shots that photographers have taken of homes being sold. I will point out the good points or the weak points of the individual pictures so you get the idea of what will work best and what will not.

If you have concrete near the home, hose it down first with water so that when you shoot the exterior picture, you get the reflections from the wet pavement to enhance the sparkle of the home. Be sure all the lights are on if shooting at or near dusk or at night.

If there is a nearby hill or higher place you can go to get a shot of the house plus an attractive background, do so as in the previous photo. The lake and surrounding mountains near this home are a big asset to it and assets like these should be included in a shot whenever possible.

Feature the home that resides on or near a cul-de-sac. That is an asset. While you're at it, include a great sunset view if you can. But don't do a distant shot like this if it diminishes special features that the home contains near the front door, because you just can't lose too much detail of what the home looks like from too far away.

Balance the home where you have it positioned a little above center, vertically. In this example, you can see a little more of the driveway and front yard than the sky. What's more important, the front of the house leading to the street or the sky behind it? Additionally, by placing the home slightly above vertical center, it does not appear to be falling out of the picture and is more pleasing to the eye.

Don't shoot the house when it is in the shade. Here the bright sky behind takes center stage and makes the house really difficult to see. The owner isn't selling the sky. They are selling a house and it is the house that must command all of the attention.

If the home you have staged is open and airy, try to feature that in your shots. People buy homes that look spacious to them. Keep the decorating simple and understated.

If the home has extra high walls, and especially if they feature assets like additional windows, get as low as you can get to take the shot. There's nothing wrong with lying on your stomach to get an upward trending shot of the room. Spaciousness isn't just at eye level. Spaciousness goes out and it also goes up. Try to capture that in your after shots especially for a fantastic look.

If you can get a shot from the top of the stairs, this is a great way to create a feeling of spaciousness even though the actual space may be quite small.

Avoid taking pictures that are too dark. A daytime shot of this home would be far more effective. The angle should also be adjusted to feature the entry of the home, not necessarily the garage. This would also help eliminate a tree from taking center stage.

High contrast can be used quite effectively for attracting attention. When competing with other homes, you need to present photos that grab the attention as much as possible.

Even though I adjusted the light in this picture quite a bit for reproduction, it is still very dark. You don't want people to have to struggle to see the various elements in the room. So when you're shooting a room with very little contrast or "tone-on-tone" (decorated in all one color), you have to be especially careful that you get enough contrast so it will reproduce well.

If the home includes some really special element (like this fountain) that separates it from all others, be sure to feature it. Make your pictures memorable.

This home, situated on a beautiful canal, came with a fabulous headline which read,

"LIVE ON THE WATER . . . OR WISH YOU DID. WHICH WILL IT BE?"

Don't rely solely on the pictures to sell your services. Create headlines that sizzle and sparkle and conjure up all sorts of hidden wishes and dreams. It's not just about buying or selling a house – it's about buying or selling a dream.

Your pictures should conjure up memories, forgotten fantasies and wishes, the unattainable made possible. When your services help a buyer gain an emotional connection with the home, you've done your job beautifully.

Often times track homes or divisions have names that captivate the heart, such as Seabridge, Renaissance, Indian Oaks, Arboreta. Include the descriptive names of the developer. This helps you romance the home and how you staged or redesigned it for your client. This is far better than referring to the home as 124 Dirtpile Road. Just kidding, but you get the point, right?

Turn all the lights on when you shoot inside, even if it is still day time. The sparkle and shadows that lights will create against the ceiling and walls will add depth to your pictures and give the room a warmer feeling.

Don't let the trees grab all the attention. Look for angles that diminish this type of feeling you see here. Better to try and get two sides of the house than to make the trees the focal points.

Clean and uncluttered works very well every time. When staging a home and addressing the outside, look for ways to unify the landscaping and de-emphasize anything that blocks view of the house. Yards can be changed, but the house will remain as is primarily.

Shooting straight on may get the whole front of the house in the shot, but in this case all one seems to notice is the large tree right in the front looking a bit out of place and in the way. By altering the angle you can keep this from happening to your pictures. By moving more to the left, the tree would not be planted right in the middle of the shot, and you'd still be able to see the garage. It just would be more pleasing to the eye compositionally if the shot were taken at an angle.

This picture was shot at sunset by the photographer, which is nice if the picture is shown in color. But it was much darker than I'm showing here and so far away, one finds it extremely difficult to see much of anything. I understand this is a ranch-style home, but it doesn't do that much good if you can't see it and have to strain at that.

Don't make people take extra effort to view your pictures.

When you can, try to include two sides of the house in your picture. This creates more interest and depth and makes the home look much larger than it might be. It's usually pretty obvious as to which of the two sides of the house gives you the best photo when shot together with the front.

Here is a typical empty room. The stager captured one wall and part of another one and the lighting fixture. Capturing the lighting fixture is important so that when you see it again in the after shot, you know immediately that it is the same room.

Next is a kitchen with an ugly bare spot where a refrigerator would normally be placed. But because the stager or homeowner wasn't going to bring in a refrigerator while the house is showing, the stager treated the area cleverly to minimize the negative effect.

By showing pictures like these two, you prove that you are a problem solver and that you know how to minimize any defects in the home without spending a great deal of money, if any money at all.

Demonstrate how furniture from one room can be better utilized in another room or in a different place in the same room to give a professional arrangement. In the after shot above, there was no rhyme or reason for why the buffet was

placed where it was. Now it looks fabulous and serves a purpose.

I'm showing you pictures from portfolios of some of my students because I want you to see that anyone, and I do mean anyone, can be a home stager or re-designer. It takes the right amount of knowledge, but as you can see, ordinary people just like you have started their own businesses from taking my courses and have pulled together the images to go into their own portfolios and on their websites. You can too.

Bathrooms are quite easy to do unless toilets, vanities or shower/tubs need to be replaced. But when the bath is in excellent condition, all that is needed is a personal touch – some accessories placed in the right places. Quite easy. See how much more appealing the bath is now.

There will be rooms that might need simple cosmetic adjustments and improvements, such as this bedroom. Here the stager concentrated on the comforter and pillows for the bed. By layering the pillows and creating a strong horizontal line, she not only made the bed look more appealing but she made it look wider too.

Watch out when you've got shutters or drapes that are open in the background as you'll get a picture that looks like this. Close the shutters or drapes before taking your pictures (these are both before pictures) so that the furnishings in the foreground can be seen. (These are both "before" pictures.)

Here is the re-designed room later in the day. But notice that the plates from lunch were left on the counter when the shot was taken. The only way this picture would be usable is if it were cropped in the front.

Here is a better picture for one's portfolio below.

This was a little girl's bedroom before the stager worked on the room. Pretty cluttered, right?

Above (top) is the after shot, but since the client wouldn't let the stager remove the little shelf (Elise), and it is way out of scale and proportion, this would be an excellent time to manipulate the picture and remove the shelf if using in your portfolio.

Now let's see what has been done to improve the picture for use in a portfolio (2nd picture). First I removed the shelf unit with the girl's name (Elise). I also removed the electrical outlet near the floor by the desk (left side). The year 2008 has also been partially removed so as not to date the picture. These are just simple adjustments you can make yourself to your digital images in a photo editing program.

It's better to remove something from the photo that jumps out at you when it is all wrong than to leave it in. I'm no photo specialist, but I've learned how to use some of the simple tools in my software to accomplish what needs to be done. You can do the same thing. It just takes a little practice and if you need help, there should be plenty of knowledgeable people around you to help you.

Look for angles that really enhance the design elements of what you've been able to achieve. Angular shots show depth better than shots that are taken straight on. They are also more interesting to look at.

Below the shades look lovely rolled half way up but they don't do much for the ability to get a good shot that is not washed in too much light.

Look for ways to show two walls at the same time. Here we have a nice shot of the dining room table staged for an open house, and it sets off the buffet in the background making it a very nice looking space.

See the spaciousness in the shot above of the same home.

I hope you're getting the idea. Each room will dictate where you need to stand to get the best picture when you're all done. Some will be easier than others.

Look for ways to get close ups and distance shots. If you're working in an open area such as this, where the kitchen, dining room and family room are not separated by walls, try to capture that feeling in your work. These are the kinds of pictures that are ideal for anyone's portfolio.

Of course, any time you have a room that feels chaotic and is extremely cluttered, it's pretty easy to make instant improvements by rearranging the furniture and accessories. This costs the home owner nothing and only requires your time to figure out a better arrangement and get everything in its proper place.

Any time your prospect can see that you've made a significant improvement to a room, they are gaining respect for you and your talents and drawing closer to doing business with you again.

This re-designer did a magnificent job in rearranging this room. By placing the sofa on an angle and moving the TV, by filling up the shelves with more accessories and changing out the scale and proportions, the room has taken on a real charm and even though there is more in the room now than before, it appears orderly and organized.

By carefully shooting your rooms before you go to work and shooting them again afterwards, it won't take you long to build enough pictures for a very impressive portfolio.

Chapter Sixteen

Using Humor

I've found that no matter what type of presentation you're doing (whether one on one or to a group), if you can get your audience laughing at the beginning, you'll have them eating out of the palm of your hand. Everyone loves to laugh and it's one of the healthiest things one can do.

Multiple decades ago, when I was in high school, I took an American history class. My teacher sat at the front of the room at the "teacher's desk" and read out loud to the class from a paperback book, which was our text book.

I was bored to tears and pulled "C's" and "D's" in the class.

My junior and senior year I had a 6'6" ex-marine for a teacher who literally loved to teach, loved the subject, and made it fun to learn and challenging too.

I pulled straight "A's" both years.

When you enjoy your students and enjoy teaching them, they will enjoy listening and learning.

Years later I studied acting for several years. I learned a very, very important concept that has stayed with me my whole career and I'll pass it on to you now.

When a person gets in front of an audience, the audience OWES the speaker nothing. They do NOT owe the speaker their attention. They do NOT owe the speaker their silence.

It is the speaker's job to interest them - to be interesting - or to be entertaining - or both.

If the speaker fails to keep their interest, it is the speaker's fault, it's not the fault of the audience.

So whether you're funny or you're not, you absolutely MUST BE INTERESTING. And it's a whole lot easier to hold their interest for a long period of time if you occasionally add something that makes them laugh.

Do some research for good one-liners that you can sprinkle throughout your speech or presentation. But open with a good joke (hopefully one that links in some way to your theme or to the person or group you are dealing with at the time).

Here are some excellent resources as of this writing that you might acquire from Amazon.

The Comedy Thesaurus by Judy Brown
1,911 Best Things Anybody Ever Said by Robert Byrne
Wild Words from Wild Women by Autumn Stephens

People will stay with you all day if you keep them laughing. Naturally, it goes without saying, that the jokes or one-liners should be "clean".
Just as important as the quality of the joke, your delivery must be good. The worst thing you can do is to TRY to be funny. When people try to be funny, the joke usually falls flat. So you just want to be sort of "dead pan" or "dry" in your delivery. Keep the joke subdued, matter-of-fact.

One of the ways people ruin jokes is by over-emphasizing the punch line, or certain words in the punch line. When you over-emphasize words you'll ruin the effect, trust me.
In acting, over emphasis is called "sing-songing the line". I'm sure you've heard people do this, especially amateur actors or presenters. So remain natural, using the same kind of natural inflections and emphasis that you'd use in the rest of your presentation. This is the best way to get your audience or prospect laughing – really laughing. Keep it dry. Keep it understated. Keep it clean.

Here's an example of something you could read in a *women's only* group that should get a good laugh, primarily because everyone can relate to it so easily, no matter what their age or gender. This was sent to me by a friend and I have no idea who wrote it, but I got a good laugh from it.

Original List: What I Want in a Man
1. Handsome
2. Charming
3. Financially successful
4. A caring listener
5. Witty
6. In good shape
7. Dresses with style
8. Appreciates finer things
9. Full of thoughtful surprises
10. An imaginative, romantic lover

What I Want in a Man, Revised List (age 32)
1. Nice looking
2. Opens car doors, holds chairs
3. Has enough money for a nice dinner
4. Listens more than talks
5. Laughs at my jokes
6. Carries bags of groceries with ease

7. Owns at least one tie

8. Appreciates a good home-cooked meal

9. Remembers birthdays and anniversaries

10. Seeks romance at least once a week

What I Want in a Man, Revised List (age 52)

1. Not too ugly

2. Doesn't drive off until I'm in the car

3. Works steady - splurges on dinner out occasionally

4. Nods head when I'm talking

5. Usually remembers punch lines of jokes

6. Is in good enough shape to rearrange the furniture

7. Wears a shirt that covers his stomach

8. Knows not to buy champagne with screw-top lids

9. Remembers to put the toilet seat down

10. Shaves most weekends

What I Want in a Man, Revised List (age 62)

1. Keeps hair in nose and ears trimmed

2. Doesn't belch or scratch in public

3. Doesn't borrow money too often

4. Doesn't nod off to sleep when I'm venting

5. Doesn't retell the same joke too many times

6. Is in good enough shape to get off couch on weekends

7. Usually wears matching socks and fresh underwear

8. Appreciates a good TV dinner

9. Remembers your name on occasion

10. Shaves some weekends

What I Want in a Man, Revised List (age 72)

1. Doesn't scare small children

2. Remembers where bathroom is

3. Doesn't require much money for upkeep

4. Only snores lightly when asleep

5. Remembers why he's laughing
6. Is in good enough shape to stand up by himself
7. Usually wears some clothes
8. Likes soft foods
9. Remembers where he left his teeth
10. Remembers that it's the weekend

What I Want in a Man, Revised List (age 82)
1. Breathing
2. Doesn't miss the toilet.

Having said all of this, however, there is a specific goal you should have in mind every time you make a presentation to someone, whether a single person, a small group or a large group.

The most important thing you will accomplish at any speaking event or opportunity to show your portfolio is to collect email addresses and business cards.

Many people will be interested, but perhaps don't have time that day to chat or communicate, or need more time or information to digest first. But once you've got their contact information, which they freely will give to you, you can follow up. That's where the REAL business takes place. That's also when and how you build relationships and find ways to do things FOR them for free, which then makes them inclined in some way to reciprocate.

So be sure to come away with as many email addresses, phone numbers and business cards as you can get from any situation where you are able to talk about your services.

If the group is mostly made up of older women, collect addresses as well as email address because many older seniors may never have set up an email account.

The raffle method is an age-old sure-fire method of guaranteeing that you receive everyone's business card in a large business group. Have everyone put their card in a large container from which one card will be withdrawn to win a prize.

Great Speaking Illustration

Want a funny way to communicate the effects of a totally cluttered home? Take an old outfit or a robe and sew a bunch of junky small items on the fabric – all over the fabric. If you don't use actual objects, pin on some photos everywhere, including a picture of a fireplace or a beautiful bay window or some other fabulous architectural feature common in many homes.

Walk on stage or before your audience wearing the overly cluttered robe or outfit and ask your audience to imagine that your outfit or robe was a home. Ask them to find the most outstanding feature on the outfit. You should get a good laugh. Ask them if they think this outfit or robe would sell in a store the way it is. Of course they will say, "No way".

Then you simply relate the problems of clutter on the robe with clutter in the home. Everyone will get the point in a very humorous, yet compelling, illustration of what home staging and interior redesign is all about.

Making Friends in the Home

Whenever you're in a prospect or client's home, try to befriend their pets and children. Even pets are considered family members by their owners and they feel comfortable with consultants who appreciate their pets. Be friendly to their children as well. If they have small children, get down to their level when speaking to them. Children will love you for it and speak well of you when you are not there.

Chapter Seventeen

Getting All the Testimonials and Letters of Reference You Can Use

When you're self employed, it is your responsibility to get yourself in front of new prospects on a regular basis or your business will not last very long. But realize that every time you are meeting with a prospect, it is equivalent to going on a job interview.

Think back to when you were employed by someone else and when you went for your job interview. What did you take with you? I hope and assume you took a resume with you. This is what most people do, unless they are looking for low paying, dead-end jobs like at a fast food restaurant.

Did you fax over the resume? Hopefully not. Did you email your resume? Hopefully not. I hope you were smart enough to hand carry your resume with you.

Well, think about every meeting you have with a potential client as going on a job interview with resume in hand. Only this time we'll be calling it a portfolio.

If you were applying for a "left brain" position with a company, your resume would be full of facts and figures. But this is a visual business, so your resume turns into a portfolio, which includes a resume or bio about you, but goes a whole lot farther.

Getting people to actually sit down and write you a testimonial or letter of reference can be difficult, depending on the person. Some people will naturally be happy to help you and they will do so immediately.

Others will take prodding.

In order for them to do anything at all, it's good to give them a good reason for why you're asking them for this favor.

So here is a brief script I suggest you use to put more importance on their cooperation and give them a stronger motivation to follow through.

I go out on a job interview every time I call on a new prospective homeowner or real estate agent. Who would ever go out on a job interview without a reference letter? This gives me the power to hire or fire myself every day. Please help me get hired.

Do you see how much more effective this type of request is than one where you just ask them for a testimonial?

If the person is extremely happy and enthusiastic, and you surmise that they have good follow through skills, then I would ask them to write the letter within 24 hours and send to you. I'd give them a self-addressed stamped envelope to use to send it to you. However, the best method is to make arrangements to pick up the letter at a specific time the next day – this encourages them to follow through.

By making an appointment to pick up the letter personally, you will help seal the deal and it will be far more likely they will comply than if you leave no deadline.

But if you elect to give them an envelope to use, be sure you put a stamp on it. Don't make them pay to send it to you.

Lastly, if the person's response is more lukewarm or you suspect they aren't the type to give you a letter of reference within the next 24 hours, you'll find a one page form at the end of this book to use.

This is for a testimonial, as opposed to a Letter of Reference. You hand the form to them right after they pay you and ask them to write whatever they wish with regards to their experience of working with you.

Some may choose to write something critical. You have to recognize that there are some people who will never be pleased with anything, no matter how well done. They are just highly critical people by nature.

Don't read what they wrote in front of them. Give them time to write while you collect all your gear so you're not making them feel uncomfortable.

Thank them for taking the time and say, "I always appreciate feedback, especially if it helps me improve my services and skills." Read the testimonial later in private.

If you receive some negative feedback, send them a thank you card immediately and express gratitude for their comments. Tell them you will weigh them carefully in your future endeavors and wish them well.

If you receive favorable comments, send them a thank you card immediately and express gratitude for what they wrote.

No matter what, always send a thank you card immediately to every client and every prospect. Treat everyone in the way you would want to be treated. Many, many people have received new business simply by sending a thank you card because so few businesses take the time to do so.

Include Your Certification Proof

If you have completed certification, you probably received some sort of certificate of completion. You should photocopy this and include in your portfolio as part of your documentation. Here is an example of one of ours, which is one of the most prized certifications in the industry because it requires proof of knowledge and talent before it is ever awarded to someone.

Copies of other achievements, nominations, plaques and assorted recognition can also be valuable to include, even if it was achieved in a different industry. It shows that you are an accomplished person and a person of action. Prospects will love to see that type of evidence in your background.

Chapter Eighteen

Using Success Stories Effectively

Most of the time, the best way to use success stories is in the natural conversations you will have with your prospects and clients. You want to sprinkle some of your stories into your presentation, but be careful not to overdo a good thing.

Do not mention names of the clients unless you and the prospect have an acquaintance in common. You don't want to acquire a reputation for "name dropping".

But if you're in tune with your prospect and listening and asking probing questions, you'll find plenty of opportunities to verbally illustrate a point or two by telling them how you solved someone else's similar problem. You can relate funny stories, difficult stories or easy stories.

Everyone loves stories and they help you personalize your service. Since you haven't used any client's name in telling your stories, your prospect will automatically know that if you ever tell a story about them, you will not use their name either.

Rather than plan specific places to insert stories, I much prefer to let them enter my conversation during the natural flow of exchanges with my prospect.

But when you're preparing your portfolio, you might also think about places within your presentation materials where you could insert a good story, illustrated by your photos and the client's testimonial or letter of reference.

I wouldn't advise telling more than 3 separate stories, spaced out throughout a presentation. Just give the barest of facts. Don't go on and on and on. Your prospect will appreciate you giving an illustration, but talking about other people can become quickly boring to them.

Tell the facts that will illustrate a point and then move on.

The Power of Stories

Telling stories about your former projects or current ones is a powerful way to interest your prospect, describe what you mean, and get them to "see" differently. Telling stories gives word pictures to your prospects and clients and helps them truly understand your objectives.

It's quite easy to understand the effectiveness of showing before and after pictures. We've already discussed this. But have you thought about the power of telling before and after stories?

Words are very powerful, particularly if they create word pictures in the mind of the listener. Carefully worded stories, full of descriptive adjectives and adverbs, with action verbs, will be remembered by your prospects. They will not only be remembered, they will be passed on to their family and friends and co-workers.

There is a passage in the Old Testament that says something to the effect, words can actually "descend like dew, like showers on new grass, like abundant rain on tender plants" (Deuteronomy 32:2).

Other passages from the Old and New Testament (The Bible) teach us that when used sparsely – succinctly – words carry *great meaning*. Words actually *give light*. Words give understanding to those who don't yet understand: They prove you're a person of knowledge, will be heeded when they are spoken *quietly* and *humbly*.

Proverbs 16:24 says that pleasant words are a *honeycomb*, sweet to the soul and healing to the bones. What a great image.

So your words are very important. And words woven together form the stories you will tell.

In the beginning of your business you aren't likely to have any stories of your own. But that's perfectly OK. You can tell the stories which other people have experienced with almost as much power. You don't claim them as your own.

Instead of saying "I did this . . ." or "I did that . . ." you say, "The stager on this project did this . . . ." or "The re-designer of this room did that . . . ." You don't have to identify who the stager or re-designer was. Many people won't even pick up on which consultant did the actual work because they become so engrossed in the story itself.

So stories will help you make your case more effectively than virtually anything else you can say. Stories coupled with great before and after pictures will be part of every great portfolio. You can even print out your stories to leave behind with a prospect that isn't ready to make a decision yet. Your words will work for you or against you. They carry that much power. A wise consultant will work hard when first entering a person's home to look for one or two elements that can be used to compliment the owners. A well placed compliment, genuinely delivered, will go very far to warm up a prospect for the rest of the time you're in their company.

Many years ago a relative of mine moved to the mountains and bought a gorgeous home nestled in the middle of giant trees. The home was on a narrow winding road and the closest neighbors were a stone's throw away.

Another relative of mine visited them in the mountains for a day or two. This person is not known for being very complimentary, especially when in a home that is more beautiful and up-to-date than her own. So the entire time she was in this fabulous mountain home, she never offered one compliment on the home, nor the way it had been decorated.

About 6 months later, I visited the home, along with my family. We had gone to the same mountains and rented a cabin for a week's vacation. One night we were invited over to my relative's home for dinner.

The moment I entered the home I began to rave about how beautiful it was. They had done a very nice job of decorating and arranging it, and I have to admit I was a bit jealous, as it was newer than my own home.
We shared a very enjoyable meal and conversation was enthusiastic and heartwarming.

A few weeks later, I happened to talk to my relative, who told me that his wife had enjoyed the evening so much with us, that we were welcome to come back any time in the future, and even go there and stay for a week, even if they were not going to be home.

Now how many people do you know who would invite you to stay in their home without them being present? No other person in my family had ever been extended such an invitation.

I'm convinced that the reasons I was so favorably remembered was because I took the time to appreciate the home and I expressed that appreciation sincerely and lavishly, opening the door to a warm, generous and close relationship. I never took them up on the offer, because that's not my style, but I did appreciate getting it.

Stories work.

Stories help you illustrate a point.

Stories get remembered and passed around.

Everyone Has Stories

I've already said that the stories you tell don't have to be your own stories, but it's better if they are. Initially you won't have stories of your own, most likely, but you then borrow stories from other people. However, whether you use your own stories or borrow from others, you want the stories to be truthful; you want them to be factual; you want them told genuinely; we want them to relate (if possible) to the topic.

I just told you a story that doesn't relate to staging or redesign, at least not obviously. But it was a story that illustrated a point, so effective stories don't always have to relate in obvious ways, but of course they are better if they do.

To give you some examples that you could use, here are some actual stories submitted by members of my free discussion forum. I'm choosing their stories over my own because they are located in various places all over the country, so you'll get broad based stories, not ones isolated to a particular locality.

I want you to notice that the stories, quoted verbatim here (except for some minor spelling corrections), usually tell you some "before" facts as well as some "after" facts. These are the best kinds of stories to use when showing your portfolio, whether you have pictures to demonstrate the points or not.

Story 1

My home was on the market for 10 months - all with neutral colors on walls, carpet etc. I had hardwood floors and updated bathrooms but no furniture. We took it off the market and I staged the whole house. It was on the market for less than a week and we received 3 offers - one for full asking price!

Story 2

A client with 3 young kids had a nicely updated split-level in an upscale community. Her neighbor was also thinking about selling - direct competition for size, style and location. Splits are the least desirable style in the Boston area, so she knew it would be a challenge. She said her real estate agent was going to list it at $589 K, she was hoping to get more but also needed the quick sale. I did some research in public records and found that most of the homes in her highly desirable school district had sold for over $950K, so she needed to highlight that to her broker as a key marketing point. Then we reworked her lower level playroom, made the master an adult sanctuary (instead of yet another playroom with kids stuff everywhere), repositioned drapes and carpets, bought slipcovers for tired sofas, created an elegant entry and put a lot of things in storage. We turned her haphazard, playroom /grad-student lounge look into an inviting stylish polished home - in two days. Her husband was amazed at the transformation. The broker came back, and based on the data I had provided, along with the professional look and quality of the materials now highlighted throughout the house, listed the house for $659K, and got 3 above asking offers that day. My client is now in her dream home, and recommends me to everyone she knows (so does the broker!!).

And the neighbor's house? Her neighbor listed their house for $659K as a FSBO, and 7 months later its down to $529K, but then again - she didn't want to hire me!!! She thought she could do a better job herself and didn't see any value in my services at the time. I think her $130,000+ loss proves that point, don't you?

Story 3

The second example was a client who had an old 4 bedroom farmhouse on a very busy main road. He needed to sell it to retire out of state. He was attached to the house, but knew it needed "something" to help it sell after sitting on the market for 2 years. He had dropped the price from $475 to $399K. I did some research, and found that the house would qualify as mixed use commercial space. We cleared out most of the first floor rooms, took down all the old draperies and let in the light, turned the second floor into flexible living space with 2 bedrooms and a living area. He had paved a lot of his outdoor space so his kids could ride their bikes away from the main road - I told him that made it a great potential parking area! We turned the negative of a too-busy road for a private residence into a positive for a high visibility commercial space - his private home is now a flourishing funky florist. His broker had tried to talk to him about changing the zoning, but he hadn't been able to think about it as anything other than a house, until I came in and showed him how someone else might look at it, and after two years of no sale - he was ready to change his mind set. Oh yes, and it was only on the market for 30 days, and at close to the original asking price of $475K. Once again, happy broker, happy seller, and happy buyer - and the community gets a new florist!

These stories go to prove that an outside eye can influence the seller and the broker as to the potential of a property, and the increased dollar value of a re-designed home is significant. What is ultimately a low cost & minimal time investment (typically under $2000 and less than 2 days) produces up to a 20% increase in value almost every time. So, go armed with public record data for past comps, listing service data for current comps, your decorator tool kit and help your broker and seller make the most of their product!

Story 4

I have done 2 vacant homes in my new business. The first was a brand new townhouse which had been on the market for 6 months. The realtor paid for the staging and actually purchased the furniture and accessories (as there are 4 more units almost ready to sell). It sold in one week!

The second home hasn't been so fortunate. It's a fabulous 4000+ guest house/pool house place which the realtor had painted all gold. The biggest drawback to this place is marble - marble floors through the entire first floor, up the stairs, hallway and even the MASTER BEDROOM! The kitchen has dark marble on the floor and even one whole wall. Cold! It is still on the market five weeks later, and that is the comment everyone makes. Too much marble.

I wanted to do more staging, but the realtor felt she couldn't afford it (the homeowner wouldn't help). We staged most of the main rooms, but not the huge formal dining room or patio, both of which would have helped. Also, even though I brought in quite a few rugs, there should have been more, especially in the master bedroom, which only has a bed.

So I've learned to really focus on camouflaging the strong negatives, as they take away from the positives.

Story 5

My statistics so far is about 3 weeks; but that is an average. Unfortunately, staging is only part of the whole package, since the price of a house and the agent can have a lot to do with how fast it sells.

I think the job I am the most proud of is the house that had been on the market for 12 months with only one really low offer. It was vacant by the time I got to it, and with one day of staging magic, the owners received 3 offers in 3 weeks. They were so happy, since they had been making two house payments for nearly a year! One of the offers was from Japan, and the potential buyers intended on buying the house based on the photos, without ever having seen it in person!

My worst case so far: I've had one house that stayed on the market for nearly 4 months after staging, (this was after it had been on the market for 6 months before being staged). The reason for not selling faster? Right after I staged it, that same day, a potential buyer looked at it, wanted it, but had to sell their house first. As a result, the agent never changed out the old photos for the 'new and improved' staged photos, thinking these people would buy the house. They couldn't sell theirs, and eventually another buyer came along.

I also had a house that sold in one week after staging (new to the market, but the price was low, so that had a lot to do with it) and I think the house I staged last week received an offer the next day, before it was even on the market (another one where I think the price was lower than it could be).

And a tip for all the home stagers: Put a good quality topiary in nearly every room; they look really modern and expensive without drawing too much attention to themselves.

Learn to Tell Your Stories Well

So as you begin to do projects, your own stories will develop and grow. But to help you organize them and make sure you are formulating them in the most powerful ways, use the following form to jot down some notes, facts, descriptive words, action words – the kinds of things that will make your stories truly come alive and reach out and touch your prospects.

BEFORE FACTS	AFTER FACTS

As you get more accustomed to telling your stories, you'll naturally come up with better ways to express your feelings. Better stories will eventually replace weaker stories. You'll refine them. You'll shorten them. You'll develop short versions and long versions. As long as your prospect appears engrossed in your story, tell it to the end. But if you notice your prospect seems anxious or disinterested in any way, then move on quickly to something else. Later evaluate your story to see if it fit the situation or if there is a more effective way you could have told it. Don't just assume your story is powerful. Make sure it is.

You'll have to create sensible transitions from one topic to another using connective phrases and sentences. Listen to the questions your prospects are asking you and this will often dictate when you show pictures, when you tell stories, when you look at the home, when you share your bio and testimonials.

If you're often responding to the prospects questions and asking them more questions to get the information you need, you'll find the whole discussion will progress in natural and comfortable sequences. One presentation for one prospect may very well start and proceed in a different way than ones that have gone before or ones that are yet to be held.

What I'm saying is that there is no right or wrong way to work with your portfolio. If you concentrate on being friendly, being positive and encouraging, asking probing questions, listening carefully to answers, answering their questions fully, you'll discover the whole process is easy and natural and quite fun as well.

Later if you find there are important segments that have been overlooked or forgotten, you can always say things like, "Oh, before I leave, let me be sure to share my bio with you." Or "That reminds me, I want to leave you with a list of my current testimonials."

If time is short, you want to deal with the most important aspects of your portfolio first, and then leave information with them for their quiet perusal after you have gone.

Time Factors

When you set your appointment with a prospect, be sure to clear a specified amount of time with them and get them to agree to give you that amount of time. There is nothing worse than having 30 minutes of prepared "show and tell" and arrive at a meeting only to be told they have 10 minutes to give you.

If a prospect can't or won't give you the amount of time you need, don't set the appointment. I've found after years and years of being in business as a consultant, that if someone will not give you the amount of time you need, they are not really serious. When going on a referral appointment, all you should need is about 10-15 minutes, but if the appointment is in the home for a possible consultation or actual project, you don't want to waste time with a non-serious prospect.

So determine how much time you really need, add a little extra to the length, and ask your prospect up front to grant you that much time. A prospective client that is a good target will usually rise to your expectations, but they have to know what those expectations are.

Be respectful of your prospect's time. Don't repeat yourself and don't drag things out.

When preparing your materials, it's good to have more than you need, then edit out the lesser important items. Try to put yourself in your prospect's shoes and ask yourself along the way, "Is this really important? If I was the prospect, would I want to hear this information? What does it have to do with the prospect? How will it benefit the prospect?"

If you cannot answer "yes" to the above questions, then it might be a good idea to remove them from your portfolio or your verbal presentations.

If your prospect relates a problem along the way that has little or nothing to do with the topic, make a mental note and come back to it later by saying, "You know, I might have a solution to recommend to you about that. I'll share it with you at the end. Is that ok?"

When you've finished your business, then come back and discuss the problem that your prospect brought up. The reason for dealing with it later is that you don't want extemporaneous subjects to interfere with the flow of why you are there in the first place.

You'll discover very quickly that you will develop a flow of thought, a flow of speech, a flow of ideas during your presentation. Preserve that by telling the person that you're not dismissing the importance of their question, but that you'd like to remain focused on the present topic and that you'll deal with that question or problem at the conclusion. Most people will be very accommodating about this.

Chapter Nineteen

How to Use Your Portfolio

When you first arrive at your prospect's home, be sure to look around for some immediate asset which you can speak positively about. Be genuine. Be sincere. But no matter what the home looks like, there should be something you can point out to compliment.

Keep control of the meeting. Remember you are interviewing them to make sure that there is a need for your services and that you are the best choice for them to select as a stager or re-designer. It's not just about them deciding to hire you, but it's also about you deciding whether they are the type of client you wish to do business with and that you can absolutely make an improvement in the situation. So try to set the agenda yourself so that the end result will be a win/win for all parties.

I will usually ask to talk where there is a table, such as in the dining room. It's important to meet in a more neutral area of the home, one that resembles the setting of a business office. This helps convey the impression that you are a business professional. It also gives you a table surface to place your materials and portfolio on so that you can easily display what you want and share your materials for everyone to see.

Keep in mind at every stage of the game that, as a home stager, you'll want to focus your seller (or agent) on developing the eyes of a potential buyer. Until they can disassociate themselves from the home, by looking at it not as a home but as a house, they will have difficulty getting the home ready to sell.

As you're showing your before pictures, ask them questions like:

1. Where do you think the buyer's will look first when they see this room? Where did you look first?
2. What will stand out to buyers? What stood out to you?
3. What will make buyers want to stay in this room? What will make them want to leave?

Now direct their attention to the room you're in (assuming you are in the home to be sold). Now ask them:

1. Where will buyers look first when entering this room?
2. What will stand out to buyers in this room?
3. What will make buyers want to stay in this room?
4. What will make buyers want to stay in this home?
5. Have you visited any of the homes in the area that are for sale?
6. Have you considered any homes that might be in foreclosure where banks are offering deep discounts?
7. How do you feel your home compares to other homes of equal size and price in the area?
8. What do you feel are your home's greatest assets?
9. What do you feel are your home's greatest liabilities?
10. Have you thought about the top three items most in need of change? What are they from your perspective?
11. Do you think your perspective will equal that of a potential buyer? Why or why not?

Using probing questions such as the ones listed in this chapter (and others I have listed in my other books), you're not giving away your expertise, but you're helping to train the seller to look at their home differently than they have in the past. Then later, when you are hired (hopefully), as you start to show them what changes need to be made, you can refer back to these questions and their answers, reminding them that all changes made will be geared to attracting buyers who will want to stay in the rooms and stay in the home and then make an offer on the home.

Going Outside Too

Another important step to take as a home stager is to take your prospects out front and take them across the street where they can see from a distance what the home looks like. Ask them, "What do you see that might be a problem for someone seeing your home for the first time?" You just may find them saying things like, "Oh, I didn't realize those plants were that big. They need to be cut back." or "Wow, the place sure looks dark and uninviting suddenly." You can easily reinforce what they are already seeing on their own. Chances are most other professionals will not take a step like this. But because you did, and they internalized something important, it will help separate you from the crowd and get you hired.

What If the Situation Does Not Allow You to Show Your Portfolio?

Not to worry. In fact in many situations it can be even better for you if you simply plan on leaving your portfolio behind for them to preview at their convenience without the pressure of you being there. Remember I wrote earlier about the importance of having many sets of your portfolio so that you can circulate them continually.

If you're very busy listening to your prospects, getting to know their children and pets, asking questions, touring the home, taking them outside as well as inside, discussing their needs and wants in full, you'll find that the time quickly slips away and you still haven't gotten to any kind of presentation.

This may be the best scenario of all. While it means you'll need to return to their home on another day to retrieve your portfolio, it provides them a way to start to get to know you while you are gone. You see, it can be very uncomfortable for some people to sit through a formal presentation. It just smacks of "salesmanship" which we all tend to naturally try to avoid.

Some people may ask to see your portfolio, so by all means show it and explain it. But if the situation does not arise naturally, then don't try to force it. When things begin to wind down, you're going to say something like the following to them:

"Bob and Carol, I know I've taken up a lot of your time so far and I want to be sensitive to your family and your other scheduled events. So rather than take up more time now, I'd like you to take a day or two and get to know more about me and what I have to offer you by leaving my portfolio with you to peruse at your leisure after I'm gone. I'll be happy to set a date and time with you at your convenience and come back to pick it up. It's got a lot of background information on me personally, but it also has some great tips for selling a home and I think you'll find it really valuable to browse later. Would that be ok with you?"

No one is going to say "no". As a matter of fact, they will probably breathe a sigh of relief knowing it's time to take the kids to soccer practice, or knowing their favorite TV show is about to start. You know, if you just put your self in their shoes now and again it becomes quite easy to see what you should do in every situation.

This is really important. It's not just about treating other people the way you would want to be treated – as important as that is. But it both unfair to them and certainly unfair for you to try to make a presentation to someone who is distracted or pressed for time and only paying half attention to you and your presentation.

All kinds of things can happen. Kids can return home from school and calamity happens. TVs get turned on. Dogs are running through the house. Babies wake up and start crying. You name it.

So realize in advance that anything can disrupt a perfectly good plan or prevent your "show and tell" from ever happening. Not to worry. You've always got a spare portfolio with you and you are prepared for any eventuality. Or at least you will be from now on.

Never Be in a Hurry

While you always want to be respectful of your prospect's time, never be in any hurry to get to one aspect or another of your presentation. Time is on your side. Remember, you're here in their home to first build a relationship with them – a friendship if you will. That takes time. It usually takes more than one visit to reach a point of trust and mutual respect that will lead to business. Don't force the situation. You can't force a romance to happen faster than both parties are willing for it to happen. The same is true in staging and redesign.

Allow the relationships to build naturally. To force things only makes you appear cold, calculating and interested in your desires and needs above theirs. You also need time to evaluate them and decide whether you even want the project or not.

Just because you are together in their home, and the original idea is for you to be hired to help them with their home, that doesn't mean that you have to take on the project at all. As a matter of fact, if you sense that your personalities and styles are not meshing, it is better for them and it is better for you if you pass up the opportunity to work with them. Instead refer them to your competition. What, you say? Give my competition business? Never!

You know everyone has a different personality and style. Your prospects might love working with your competitor and be very grateful for being referred to them. Naturally you don't disclose why you are referring them to someone else other than to say something like, "You know I can see your home is going to need a little more attention than my schedule will allow. Will it be alright with you if I have one or two other local stagers call you if their schedule is open?"

Your prospect will appreciate the fact that you are not taking a project on that you cannot give your full attention (or heart). Your competition will be happy for the referral (most likely). And you just may find yourself getting a return referral from your competitor when you least expect one and need it the most.

By bringing in another stager or re-designer to the home you are helping a homeowner that isn't right for you and this is always good business. It's not their fault and it's not your fault. This is just a part of business and a part of being a member of the human race.

Leave With Their Contact Information

Always leave your portfolio behind even if you've had a chance to show it to them while you are there. People love to look things over calmly and take their time to discuss and evaluate you and their reactions to you privately. Allow them that luxury.

But don't leave their home without all of their contact information (phone, email and/or fax). And be sure and set a date and time for you to return to pick up the portfolio.

When you get back home or to your office, send them an email thanking them for the meeting and stating again that you will return to pick up the portfolio. Save the actual thank you "card" for after you pick up your portfolio.

It's best to allow them at least 24 hours to 48 hours before returning. You don't want them to feel unduly pressured to look over your portfolio immediately but on the other hand you don't want to give them too much time either. Many people are procrastinators and will wait until the last moment no matter how much time they are given.

So if you are at your first home visit on Saturday, don't try to pick up the portfolio until Tuesday. That should be sufficient time for them to browse through it and get to know you better, see what you have accomplished, get the tips you promised were contained within and be ready to talk to you again.

I guarantee you that if you have given people a pressure-free way to browse your portfolio, when you return they will probably greet you like a friend that they have known for a long time. It is just human nature to do this. And that puts you oh so much closer to getting hired.

If they have come to appreciate you for where you grew up, or your family, your pets, your children, your past accomplishments or whatever helped them feel more comfortable with you and feel like they have known you for some time - it will all be extremely beneficial to you.

And if you're one of those people who is afraid to make formal presentations in the first place, this should be a very freeing moment for you. I have just released you from all the pressure to become a good speaker. You will be letting your portfolio speak for you while you're gone.

I guarantee you that your competition is probably not operating this way. If they are and you are not, it will explain why they have been getting the business and you have been losing out. So whether you approach your prospects where they work for a referral interview or you approach them at their home directly, use your portfolio to "make the case" for you. It is a powerful tool. Once you begin using your first one you will wonder why you never made one before.

Continue to gather material for your portfolio. From time to time refresh it so that your pictures and bio and letters of reference are always up to date. Ask family and friends to look over what you've pulled together and give you feedback as well. Continually strive to improve the power of its contents.

Keep Your Portfolios in Your Car

Put a box on the back seat of your car and keep your extra portfolios in the box. Be sure to use a cover on the box to keep the sun off them. Never lend out a faded book. If the binding is plastic or leather, keep a sheet of cardboard or piece of fabric between them to prevent sticking in hot weather. Don't put them in your trunk, your office or your home where you're sure to forget them. You'll be traveling a lot, so keep them where you'll see them every day.

Leave your portfolios with home owners, your spouses' co-workers, your family members, your neighbors, real estate agents and brokers, home builders, appraisers, bankers and loan officers, all businesses with whom you do business, all people you share referrals with. Enlist the help of anyone willing to give it to you. Attend open houses in your community and leave your portfolio there (with the permission of the attending agent, of course).

Virtually the whole world is ripe to learn about you and your business. But it will never be able to find out about you unless you get out there and let them know you exist, what you can do for them and how to reach you. It begins and ends with you.

Chapter Twenty

Presentation Cases

There are many different ways to put all your materials together. Later on I'll show you examples of some of my own materials and some products I've created that you can get if you like. But here are a few other ideas and sources you can consider as well.

Of course, one of the most important considerations is how you will "house" all your materials. Will you want something small and easy to carry or will you want something larger for use with a small group. You may decide you need more than

one type of portfolio which will give you options on which one is more suitable to use at any given time.

Here are some of the more typical cases that consultants have used successfully over the years.

Simple folders can be acquired at almost any office supply store and are probably the least expensive. These are good for distributing smaller portfolios to leave behind with a prospect, or to leave at an open house for a project that you completed.

The desktop easel is very handy when sitting at a table or someone's desk and walking them through your presentation. This type of portfolio can also be left behind for an open house or to sit on a table in the entry or perhaps on a  kitchen counter where agents and potential buyers will easily see it and can browse through it on their own.

This type of portfolio usually requires full size sheets in a landscape format (horizontal) so that as the pages are flipped they are easily viewed. In this format, you'll only want to put your message on the front side of each page as you don't want people to have to turn it from side to side to see what is there. This type of portfolio is also very handy to use at trade shows. It will stand on its own quite nicely and some people refer to it as a "flip chart".

If you want a portfolio that is more portable, then consider something like the following. These are actual cases that come with handles and zippered enclosures. Artists often use these types of cases but a consultant can also make very good use of them. The insider pages are usually clear plastic "sleeves" with metal spiral type bindings. You just slip your literature in the plastic "sleeves". Choose either a portrait (vertical) format or a landscape (horizontal) format, but don't mix the two together if you want the greatest ease in sharing it with someone to view.

Again, most local office supply stores carry an assortment of these types of cases. You'll also find them at your local art supply store as well.

For sources on the internet, just do a search under "portfolio cases" in your favorite search engine, adding in your city and state so that the results are local to you.

You can get most anything from **Light Impressions**: http://www.lightimpressionsdirect.com but try your local sources first such as: Office Depot, Office Max & Staples.

Digital Presentations

You can also create digital presentations and store on CDs. These are quite inexpensive to duplicate and you can even make copies of them yourself with a CD burner.

Just name your various files by the type of document that it is. If using Microsoft Word, you can easily insert your images onto a page and wrap your text around it, just like you see here in this manual.

Type your copy on the page. Choose the "insert" link at the top of your page, then click on "picture", and then click on "from file". It will give you the option to choose the file where you have stored your pictures. Highlight the one you want and click on "insert". Your image will be displayed near your type where your cursor was. You then double click on the image and you can re-size it, move it, change it's lightness or darkness, place it behind text or along side, add a line border and a few other tricks.

This is an easy way to show your before and after pictures and you can add captions in or near the pictures to help explain them as you choose.

You can choose to have one long scrolling file for everything or break each section up into its own file.

And if you really want to get fancy, you can create a DVD portfolio, adding music to the background with a voice over explanation. But this can get costly and very time consuming to make. You really don't need to go to these lengths, particularly when you're starting out.

Creating a simple portfolio that tells your story in a powerful manner is all that you need to do. Quite often these are the best because your prospects won't get caught up in the mechanics of what you've created but will concentrate on the content and message. And that's the whole point.

Another reason for creating simple portfolios is that you don't want to convey the idea that your services will be super expensive. Unless you're presenting your services to a very, very wealthy homeowner or agent, you want your prospect to feel you are professional, but you don't want them to think that they will be forced to pay a premium fee for your services. That's another reason why I wouldn't drive up to a prospects home in a Rolls Royce (not that I have one, mind you). You just want to be careful not to convey a feeling that you're driving this big expensive vehicle because of the hefty fees you charge your clients. Moderation is best.

From this standpoint, a moderate presentation is also best. This is why, even though there is sophisticated software available to help you create a blockbuster DVD presentation, I advise against it and urge you to take the more standard, modest approaches.

As long as your presentation looks visually nice, as long as your materials are organized, as long as you tell a compelling story (featuring why you will benefit your prospect), you will have a portfolio that represents you in a powerful manner.

All else is superfluous and distracting.

Chapter Twenty-One

Layout and Design Ideas

Brochures

The typestyle and size you choose should be readable and large enough so that people don't have to strain to read it. As I've gotten older and my eyesight has diminished, I must wear reading glasses for everything.

So it's particularly annoying to try to read something in extra small type size. This book is printed in the typeface **Georgia**. I chose it because I got a little tired of my three other favorite typestyles which are: **Verdana** and **Arial** and **Tahoma**.

The reason I prefer these three normally is because they are contemporary in design and easy to read since they do not have serifs. Serifs are the little "curls" or "wings" attached to the letters as you see on this typestyle. The Georgia font (typestyle) is a little more traditional in style, but it's a refreshing difference for me to use.

If you're a wordy person, you may need to use a style that allows more characters on a line than ones that allow fewer characters. The wider a letter is, the less characters you will get on a line. Notice the difference in width between the Georgia, Verdana and Tahoma styles and the width of the

Arial style. Clearly Verdana is the widest face and Arial is the narrowest face.

Hello, my name is Barbara. (Georgia)
Hello, my name is Barbara. (Verdana)
Hello, my name is Barbara. (Arial)
Hello, my name is Barbara. (Tahoma)

In my other books, I use a 10 pt. size but in this book I'm using 12 pt. Readability is important, but obviously you want to keep your costs to a minimum and say what you need to say.

If you keep your text copy to a 10 or 12 point size, you'll find most people will be able to read without any difficulty.

Headlines and sub-headlines should be in a larger type size, and may or may not be in the same style. I prefer keeping everything in the same typestyle for unity sake, and then I alter the size of the type, and utilize bold, italics and underlining to draw emphasis to special areas.

When you're printing in color, you can also use color to a great advantage, particularly as a background color.

While you won't be able to see this book's photos in color, unfortunately, here is an example of one brochure I created to briefly highlight my courses:

Above is the cover (on far right), the inside flap (on far left) and the back (used as a mailer). The brochure is a tri-fold brochure.

You have to decide in advance what purpose your material will have. This is a mailer, but for your portfolio you're not likely to need a mailer, but something you would hand a prospect or have inserted inside a presentation folder.

Now I'll show you the inside of the brochure:

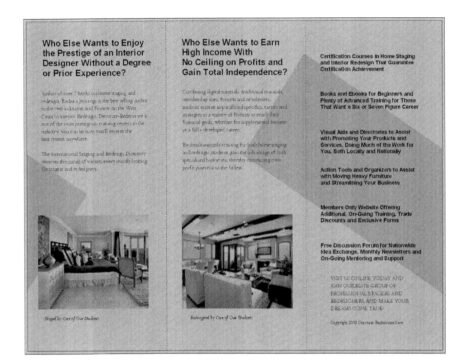

Who Else Wants to Enjoy the Prestige of an Interior Designer Without a Degree or Prior Experience?

Author of over 7 books on home staging and redesign, Barbara Jennings is the best selling author in the two industries and Number on the Web Coach in Interior Redesign, Decorate-Redecorate is one of the most prestigious training centers in the industry, you can be sure you'll receive the best system anywhere.

The International Staging and Redesign Directory receives thousands of visitors every month looking for stagers and re-designers.

Who Else Wants to Earn High Income With No Ceiling on Profits and Gain Total Independence?

Combining digital materials, traditional manuals, membership sites, forums and newsletters, students receive step-by-step specifics, tactics and strategies in a variety of formats to reach their financial goals, whether for supplemental income or a fully developed career.

By simultaneously training for both home staging and redesign, students gain the advantage of both specialized businesses, thereby maximizing their profit potential to the fullest.

Certification Courses in Home Staging and Interior Redesign That Guarantee Certification Achievement

Books and Ebooks for Beginners and Plenty of Advanced Training for Those That Want a Six or Seven Figure Career

Visual Aids and Directories to Assist with Promoting Your Products and Services, Doing Much of the Work for You, Both Locally and Nationally

Action Tools and Organizers to Assist with Moving Heavy Furniture and Streamlining Your Business

Members Only Website Offering Additional, On-Going Training, Trade Discounts and Exclusive Forms

Free Discussion Forum for Nationwide Idea Exchange, Monthly Newsletters and On-Going Mentoring and Support

VISIT US ONLINE TODAY AND JOIN OUR ELITE GROUP OF PROFESSIONAL STAGERS AND REDESIGNERS AND MAKE YOUR DREAMS COME TRUE!

Copyright 2008 Decorate-Redecorate.com

Staged by One of Our Students

Redesigned by One of Our Students

As you can see, hopefully, there is one type style for headlines and a different one for the text, with good spacing and good use of bold type mixed with regular type. Pictures always help and a colorful background strip has been added as an extra design flair.

The colors chosen for this brochure are various intensities of blue, rust, yellow, black and white. The strip is light blue, all of the type is black, the paper is white, and the rust and yellow show up in the pictures.

The key to attractive materials is simplicity and organization, just the same as staging a home. It must look unified and lead the eye in specific directions, all the while telling the story you want to tell.

Within the brochure image:
Please Place Stamp Here

It Only Takes 5 Seconds to Make a Good First Impression

For the Best First Impression, Call Us Today

Home Staging and Redesign Services

Here's another tri-fold brochure. It relies more on strong images on the cover (right side) and inside flap (left side). It too is a self-mailer. Next is the inside of this brochure (see next page).

It too relies heavily on a strong graphic image that is repeated from the front. The text is reversed out of the darker background. Reversed text is white. This is a brochure that is totally generic so that it can be used by anyone to promote their home staging services.

Notice that the layout is orderly. The text is kept to a minimum and photos capture the attention and help to strengthen the overall story.

So here you have two examples of brochures. The first uses black text on a mostly white background and the second one uses reversed text on a dark background.

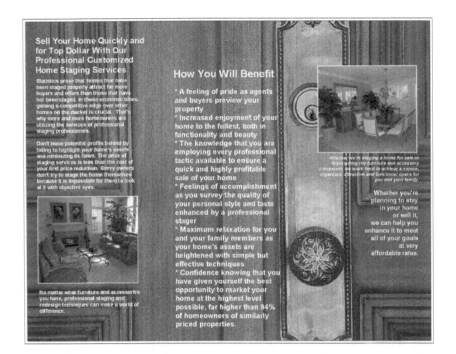

Sell Your Home Quickly and for Top Dollar With Our Professional Customized Home Staging Services

Statistics prove that homes that have been staged properly attract far more buyers and offers than those that have not been staged. In these economic times, gaining a competitive edge over other homes on the market is crucial. That's why more and more homeowners are utilizing the services of professional staging professionals.

Don't leave potential profits behind by failing to highlight your home's assets and minimizing its flaws. The price of staging services is less than the cost of your first price reduction. Savvy owners don't try to stage the home themselves because it is impossible for them to look at it with objective eyes.

No matter what furniture and accessories you have, professional staging and redesign techniques can make a world of difference.

How You Will Benefit

* A feeling of pride as agents and buyers preview your property
* Increased enjoyment of your home to the fullest, both in functionality and beauty
* The knowledge that you are employing every professional tactic available to ensure a quick and highly profitable sale of your home
* Feelings of accomplishment as you survey the quality of your personal style and taste enhanced by a professional stager
* Maximum relaxation for you and your family members as your home's assets are heightened with simple but effective techniques
* Confidence knowing that you have given yourself the best opportunity to market your home at the highest level possible, far higher than 94% of homeowners of similarly priced properties.

Whether we're staging a home for sale or redesigning the furniture and accessory placement, we work hard to achieve a serene, organized, attractive and functional space for you and your family.

Whether you're planning to stay in your home or sell it, we can help you enhance it to meet all of your goals at very affordable rates.

Use enough storytelling to make your most significant points.

Write a strong title to capture attention and peak the curiosity of the reader. Or make your headline filled with benefits so that the reader will want to keep reading.

Use bulleted lists or short paragraphs to cover your features and benefits.

Make sure your full contact information is included and give them multiple ways to contact you.

Try to balance your text material with graphics and look for a pleasing way to present your message.

Choose a reputable printer and compare prices and quality first before leaping into production.

In printing, most of the price goes into getting it ready to print, so the more copies you have printed at once, the less expensive each one becomes.

But before you would roll out a campaign, you want to order a few, verify your quality and test them out in the marketplace. Your marketplace will tell you whether your piece is powerful or not.

Letterhead

Many of the inserts in your portfolio will be printed on your letterhead, such as your Bio, your Client testimonial page, your Benefits page, your Features page and so forth.

You can design your own letterhead in Microsoft Word or some other processing program or you can have letterhead printed up or you can purchase pre-designed letterhead.

The purpose of letterhead is to help brand your image and give all your materials cohesiveness, unity and full contact information.

Your letterhead can sport a logo at the top or the bottom or it can be quite simple with no logo at all. Here are a couple of examples of letterhead using images. Notice how the letterhead, the postcards and the business cards have a "matching" design. Here are a few varieties of style for letterhead where an image is incorporated into the design.

INTERIOR REDESIGN | HOME STAGING
CONSULTATION SERVICES

Decorate-Redecorate.Com

7501 Slater Avenue, Suite C, Huntington Beach, CA 92647

(714) 963-3071 | FAX (714) 396-2771
redesign@decorate-redecorate.com
www.decorate-redecorate.com

Your letterhead is a great place to include a cover letter, a welcome letter, your bio information, a history of your company, testimonials you have received (as opposed to

Letters of Reference), and anything else you feel would be good to include.

Business Cards

Business cards are very important because you will probably use more of them than any other part of a portfolio. They are a mini-billboard about your company and can often get passed around from prospect to prospect.

You can have them match your other materials (preferred, especially when part of your portfolio) or they can have a different design depending on the product or service you are promoting with them. I actually have many types of business cards, from the serious to the whimsical.

Decorate-Redecorate.Com
Individualized Redesign Solutions for Your Home

Barbara Jennings, CRS

Phone (714) 963-3071
Fax (714) 378-2771

7501 Slater Avenue Suite C
Huntington Beach CA 92647

www.decorate-redecorate.com
redesign@decorate-redecorate.com

Here is an example of a serious card for my redesign services. I've also got a card for my cat, who thinks he's my office assistant. This one gets a lot of laughs and doesn't get thrown into the "circular file" (trash basket).

Decorate-Redecorate.Com
Interior ReDesign | Home Staging

Gadget, CCS
Marketing Mascot

(714) 963-3071
www.decorate-redecorate.com
gadget@decorate-redecorate.com

I also have a referral generating card that simply and easily reminds people that I'm always open and appreciative of their kind referrals. Here's a couple of examples of that card.

I APPRECIATE YOUR TIME

I will contact you soon to answer any questions and see how I might be of service to you.

Thank you.

P.S. I'm never too busy for your kind referrals.

I APPRECIATE YOUR TIME

I will contact you soon to answer any questions and see how I might be of service to you.

Thank you.

P.S. I'm never too busy for your kind referrals.

Folders

You'll want to place all your materials into a folder of some kind. You can buy these at any stationery store that are plain white or in assorted colors. This is the least expensive way.

Or you can have folders custom designed and printed that match your materials. This is far more professional but also far more expensive. Printed folders can be quite expensive due to the printing methods.

I'll show you a couple more examples of printed folders that have been designed to "match" some of my letterhead and business cards.

The inside of the folders have a pocket on both sides where you can slip in your sell sheets and other materials, your brochure, newspaper clippings and such. There are also slits cut into the pocket front on one side where you can affix your business card or the referral card shown previously.

Home Staging | Redesign
CONSULTATION SERVICES

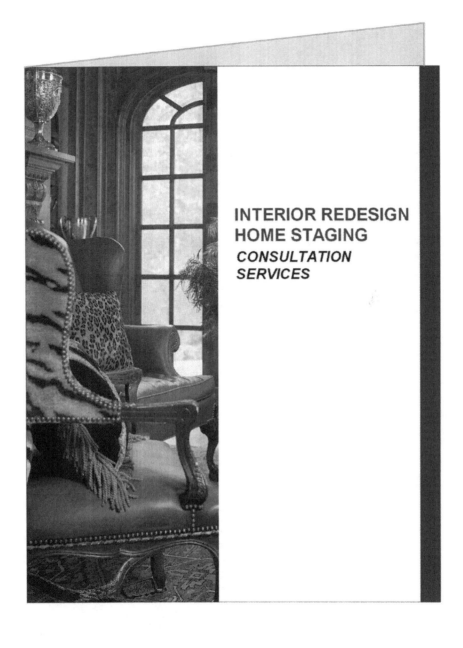

INTERIOR REDESIGN
HOME STAGING
CONSULTATION
SERVICES

Folders like these are excellent tools to use to place your materials in to leave behind with a prospect, a real estate agent, or at an open house. See my resource section at the end of this manual for how you can get some of these.

Testimonial Page

When you're brand new you won't have any testimonials. But you can get some rather quickly by offering to do some staging work and some redesign work for friends, relatives (and even your own home). Offer to do the work for free if you need to – just get some projects under your belt as quickly as possible, grab your before and after pictures from each room you do, and make sure to get written testimonials from all the home owners or agents you work for.

If the testimonials are typed on official stationery, keep them that way. If they are handwritten, keep them that way and reproduce them just as you get them.

Ask for permission to use the person's full name and city. If they don't want to be identified, use their initials. You can cut up sections or paragraphs and arrange them on your letterhead and make photocopies of the page to include in your portfolio, particularly if you've made up multiple ones for distribution.

Some people will actually read your testimonials and other people will just scan them. The important thing is to have at least one page of testimonials. You don't have to have a huge number as they won't be read anyway. But if you can eventually acquire 5-10, they will be very useful to you in gaining the confidence of your prospects.

No one likes to think they are hiring a totally inexperienced person and that they are the only one to do so. There is comfort in numbers. So when a person sees that you have been hired by other people, they automatically experience a higher comfort level.

The best testimonials will include something specific that the person appreciated about your work: your service, your punctuality, your talent, the response of potential buyers, the impressions of family members, how quickly the home sold afterwards – that sort of thing.

And if the person will allow you to show their picture (which you can take right then and there before you leave), this would be ideal for you. Having their picture beside their testimonial is more powerful than not having one.

Layout of Before and After Examples

Be sure to include some before and after pictures in your portfolio. This is one of the best ways to demonstrate your abilities without having to say a word. Remember the saying, "A picture is worth 1000 words." It could not be more true than for a stager and re-designer.

The easiest way to accomplish this is to place the before picture on the left side and the after picture on the right side. It's also good if the angle is the same in both shots, but this is not always possible.

You obviously will want to take the after shot from the best angle that shows the beauty and power of what you have achieved, which isn't necessarily the same as the before picture. For this reason, when taking all of your pictures, try to capture the room (before and after) from every conceivable angle.

Stand in all four corners and shoot the opposite two walls. Stand in the middle of one wall, and shoot the opposite wall. Grab distant shots. Grab close ups. Take your time and get plenty of shots, both before and after your work. This way you'll be able to match up the best pictures to use together to show the improvements you have achieved.

Here are a few examples of some before and after pictures taken by some of my students for their portfolios. Notice that they aren't the type of photos you might see in an interior design magazine or coffee table book. They are candid photos taken at the conclusion of a project. If some of them look dated, it's only because the home is an older home or the homeowner's furniture is dated. It does *not* mean that the photos were taken a long time ago.

BEFORE

AFTER

Notice how I have overlapped the photos with the after shot sitting on top of the before shot. You can do this for effect or because you need to for spacing. The photos could be positioned side by side or in a stair stepping fashion as you see here. Do not deliberately try to make your before picture look terrible by making it darker or fuzzier or manipulating it in any way. People are not dumb. They will notice things like that. Just take honest photographs of the room before you tackled it and afterwards. Try to shoot pictures with optimum clarity, contrast and composition. If you can include two walls in the shot (best done with a wide angle lens), this is ideal.

Notice too that there is nothing fancy about how I'm presenting the pictures. Don't feel that you've got to turn out some presentation worthy of a printing award. And don't add a bunch of extras to the presentation such as fancy backgrounds, fancy borders and such. That only detracts from what you really want your prospect to focus on.

So just print or paste your photos to a plain white or other colored background in keeping with the overall color palette of your portfolio. White is always an excellent choice because your photographs will come in a wide variety of colors and a white background will enhance all of them uniformly.

If a photo has a light background, or one side of the photo is extra light, enclose the photo with a thin black rule (line) as you see here. If using Microsoft Word, right click on the image to bring up the image toolbar.

From the toolbar, mouse over the little graphic with the horizontal lines and the dog (line wrapping) and click on the button. Choose the "tight" option from the dropdown menu. Then click on the button that has the 3 horizontal lines and choose the thickness of line you wish to add from the drop down menu. This will add a black box around your image and help define it from the background or page color.

To resize a picture, just right click on the image. In the four corners, you'll see a tiny circle appear. When you put your mouse on one of the circles and move it, you can enlarge the image proportionately or make it smaller to suit your needs.

 BEFORE

AFTER

Some people use a format like this where the before picture is shown much smaller than the after picture. Since most people are interested in the results, they don't need to see much detail in the before shot (particularly if it is an empty room).

NOTE: Here's a case where it would have been good to take out the switch plate (below on the left wall) and the wall plug from the after shot as they tend to detract. Notice too that the after shot uses a slightly different angle in order to show the wall with the artwork rather than the window.

BEFORE

AFTER

ADJACENT ROOM

Or perhaps you have pictures of a home with a particular theme and you just want to show examples of the rest of the home together with a before and after shot. By using a variety of sizes, your presentation will be more pleasing from a compositional viewpoint and more interesting too than if all of the pictures were the exact same size and presented in the exact same way. But you can do that too as shown here.

This is a more formal presentation with all of the pictures approximately the same size, similar colors, same format. For best overall look, choose colors of a similar intensity so that the presentation is unified. You don't want an odd ball in the mixture attracting too much attention to itself any more than you would want it in a room you were decorating.

You can mix landscape formats together with portrait formats, but this is more difficult to do and requires more skill to arrive at an arrangement that is pleasing to the eye.

Laying out your photographs (or images) on paper utilizes the same design concepts and rules you would use when designing a beautiful wall grouping. The only difference is that when designing on paper you are using 2-dimensional design and in a room you're using 3-dimensional design. But the theory is the same.

For design training on wall groupings and other elements, see my resources at the end of this manual.

Creating a Bound Portfolio Book

If you want a hard bound portfolio book (wrapped in linen), such as the one we created below for our Diamond Ruby trainees, you can make one yourself or purchase one of ours (which are generic). It does take time to gather your photos together, decide the sequence you want to display them in, choose a book style, write the captions and corresponding sales copy, proof read it and order one or more. But it certainly is a viable way to present your services.

Do a web search using the phrase "photo books" and you should find plenty of websites that have easy-to-upload software to create your own book. You can select the style, size and number of pages and order over the internet. I would advise purchasing just one at first to see the quality. Then you can always order more. Here is an example of one we created:

We chose a black linen cover with a cut-out in the middle showing a nicely landscaped home with the title to the portfolio: Home Staging Showcase.

The inside pages will vary in most formats you'll see available. You should be able to choose the format for each page or for a double spread as you see here.

It will be important to mention the benefits of hiring you and, of course, to show some before and after pictures. The

double photo page here (right side) is an excellent and easy way to show a before and after example.

Sometimes you may wind up with 3 views of the same room, or in this case you could put 3 before pictures on the left, a brief description of what was done, and a glorious large after shot on the right.

Don't go overboard and try to put too much in your portfolio at one time. Clients will be interested for a while but if you overload them with too many photos to look at, you will defeat your purpose – and increase the costs of the books.

Try to sprinkle meaningful benefits throughout the presentation. And don't forget to add all of your contact information at the end, and if possible at the beginning too.

Chapter Twenty-Two

Using the Web

Big Fish -- Small Pond... Simple Secrets to Hooking the Local Market

As a stager or re-designer, you have a local business -- like a service or a store -- you know you MUST have a website.

But how do you get to the top of the search results when you have to compete with every similar business on the Internet?

YOU DON'T!

You only have to compete with similar businesses in your geographic area.

Think about this as it relates to other types of businesses. Erin lives in Nashville and needs to make some color prints during her lunch break.
She hops on the Internet, does a search for "color printing Nashville," and Google Maps shows a bunch of businesses in her neighborhood.

It even shows her where they're located.

She prints out the map and heads off to get her copies done.

Erin uses the location name in her search because if she just

224

searched on "color printing" she'd get millions of useless results all over the globes.

So if you depend on local business, **use those same location-specific keywords throughout your site**. You'll get to the top of the search results for the specific market you're aiming at.

Most of your competitors won't know how to "optimize" their websites to snag those local searches. They may choose to pay in an AdWords campaign to be at the top instead, but that's very expensive and risky.

In fact, a stager based in LA is the perfect example. She commented that she's "getting terrible placement" for her site.

Well, she doesn't need to compete for her keywords with stagers all around the world, since she can't do projects *everywhere*. If she adds a geographic location to her website keywords, she's only going to face competition from the other stagers *in her area*.

With a site targeted directly at her local market, this is one stager who won't be suffering from injured rankings!

3 Easy Ways to Optimize Your Site for Local Search

So, what's involved in getting top search engine rankings for the region you want? It doesn't necessarily happen automatically and you should expect to put in some work in this area, especially if your area is highly competitive.

1. Use "geo-keywords"

First, decide on how specific to be with your location. The smaller the geographic location, the more targeted your customers will be – although, of course, you will appeal to a smaller audience.

The stager in Los Angeles would want to include "Los Angeles" and "LA." But she'll also have to say *exactly* where she is - the city, the neighborhood - even the street. People will use all those terms when they perform their searches.

And here's a tip: When you're deciding on the location keyword, **think about how *locals* would search for it.** For example, Southern California is often referred to as "SoCal". If you're targeting locals, you definitely have to speak their language and use those keywords on your site.

Make sure you **work your location keywords into your copy *and* code** wherever possible. Use them in your headlines and subheads and throughout your copy for extra impact.

One of the pages on your website could be a directions page, complete with a Google map. By using location keywords often you'll tell the search engines that your site is relevant for those words.

2. Display your address and phone number

Have your full street address on the footer at the bottom of each page and on the side navigation bar. Include a phone number with your local area code. This will give the search engines all the information they need to nail your location.

3. Get inbound local links

Search engines reward you for having links pointing to your website from other reputable sites and organizations. Local directories give you an easy way to build up your inbound links... and get your site seen by highly targeted groups of local buyers!

You can submit your site to:

- Goog411 -- http://www.google.com/goog411

- Yahoo Local Business -- http://listings.local.yahoo.com/signup/create_1.php

- TrueLocal.com -- http://www.truelocal.com/listabusiness.aspx

- Switchboard.com Yellow Pages -- http://www.switchboard.com

- Ask Local -- http://city.ask.com/city

- MSN Local/Live Maps/InfoUSA -- https://ssl.search.live.com/listings/ListingCenter.aspx

- CitySearch -- https://selfenroll.citysearch.com

- SuperPages -- http://advertising.superpages.com/spportal

- Internet Yellow Pages -- http://www.yellow.com/advertise

- Better Business Bureau -- http://www.bbb.org/membership/index.asp

- Chambers of Commerce -- http://www.chamberofcommerce.com/public/index.cfm

- Yelp.com -- http://www.yelp.com

Most of these directories offer both free and paid listings. Test out the free service before upgrading to paid to see if it works for you without having to pay any further fees. In addition, don't forget to **look for other local**

directories and networks. Search on "location name + directories" and see what comes up. More and more are appearing every day!

Here is a great resource for more information: http://www.locallytype.com/pages/submit.htm

Be search engine savvy when you're filling out your listings. Whenever possible mention keywords, area names and product names so you can be found!

Tips on Displaying Your Portfolio on Your Website

No matter what technique you use to show your work to potential clients, the most important part of your portfolio are your photographs, your benefits page and your bio.

So it naturally means that these are critical areas to cover on your website as well. Each major area should have a page devoted just to that topic:

- An About Us Page (your biography)
- A Benefits or Services Page (lists the benefits of hiring you to manage a project)
- A Contact Us Page (lists how to get in contact with you)
- A Portfolio Page (shows pictures of your previous work in the form of before and after pictures)

You can have other pages as well, but you absolutely must have the above pages at the very least.

Photos need to be optimized and displayed in low resolution. This means they can't be very big and you should only have a few on each page to reduce the downloading time when a visitor lands on the page.

So if you're going to display a lot of photos, break them up into several pages and link each page to all the other pages, either with your navigation bars, or some kind of forward and backward linking arrangement at the top and bottom of each page.

You do not have to have a fancy website with all the bells and whistles. On the contrary, simple websites are indexed better by the search engines than fancy sites with Flash. Search engines struggle with Flash. So keep this in mind - simple HTML websites are still the winners of the search engine battles. But your site does have to look nice. Gone are the days when you could get by with an ugly website (but who would want one?). So just remember, it doesn't have to be fancy, but it should look pleasing to the eye and be organized so that people can easily find what they are looking for.

For those of you who insist on something using Flash for your site, here is a source to check out that offers many different kinds of software: http://www.programurl.com Or visit: http://www.photo-mark.com/articles/database/ and read his article about doing something for free.

Online Postings at BestBiddy.Com

Best Biddy Corporation is a North American online home service marketplace with categories in **Home Design** and **Real Estate Services** where you can profile your company to enhance your ability to source customers. They are currently offering a free one year service trial with no commitment afterwards to continue. You can upload all your business information including pictures and video content to market your company. Once a consumer posts a project in your category/location, you will be notified by email and can actively bid on the project with direct communication with the prospect. The winning bid is discretionary and not based solely on price. There are other such websites with similar fee-based or free services and targeted searches should reveal a nice selection.

Chapter Twenty-Three

Conclusion

Creating a portfolio is an important aspect of being a dedicated professional. It is also relatively easy once the hurdles that have stopped so many have been pushed out of the way. Creating a portfolio allows you to see what you have accomplished so far and where you are at right now. It also allows you to plan what you want to focus on in the future. In this sense it is a landmark event that will stay as a record of what you accomplished up to any point in time. Once completed it will make it easier for you to chart the course ahead, plan your future projects and present your services in a more compelling way to each and every prospect. Your sense of purpose and direction will be enhanced once the completion of a successful portfolio is behind you.

A portfolio is also something you can go back to later on to visualize how your work has changed over time. In this sense a portfolio stands as a mark in time, allowing you to see your progression and the changes your services have undergone over the course of your career.

Countless details come into play when creating a portfolio and for this reason no two portfolios are alike. The goal of this book has been to teach you the importance of casting your seeds wherever you go, mainly with successful people who can give you great guidance on your journey and hire you whenever they see fit. Think of it as cultivating a garden.

Your seeds will be cast and sewn in good, fertile soil so that as you maintain your *garden*, and you nourish it and water it, over time your garden will grow and the roots will be deep in the soil and you'll eventually cultivate many, many blossoms (clients). And just as a garden blooms seasonally, so will your garden of contacts and prospects.

Creating a portfolio and using it to garner clients in the manner I've described for you requires, above all else, personal commitment and time. If you'll devote the time and energy to the effort, I know you'll find that it has been time and effort well spent.

Last Thoughts

Homes that have languished on the market for months or a year prior to being staged have to be reintroduced to the agents in the area as if it was brand new on the market. If the agent fails to do this, it hurts the stager's chances of seeing immediate results from their hard work. So you must still depend on the agent for the home to be priced correctly.

Let's also remember that the odds remain 50/50. Either it will sell or it won't. From that standpoint, everything is out of your hands - and out of everyone's hands, once all your work is done.

On the other side, a stager's job is to stimulate excitement in a home and if you do that, you've done your job. If you can shorten the process and if you can help the home owners avoid a price reduction, you have also succeeded. So just because a house doesn't sell right away or get multiple offers, that doesn't mean that you have failed. In every sense of the word, you've probably stimulated people to give the house a higher consideration, and if you've just done that, you've been successful.

Many factors go into the equation, not the least of which is whether the potential buyers can come up with the right down payment, or get good financing, no matter what home they are considering. But you usually will never know how many people ALMOST made an offer or wanted to make an offer and couldn't for one reason or another.

So don't get overly hung up on how fast the offers come or to what degree. Success is defined in many levels, not just those. These are issues all would do well to communicate to prospects. They are the unseen values that you bring to the table and worthy of being mentioned. It could make the difference between getting hired and not.

When redesigning for a client, your job is to make the space more functional and more pleasurable to live in. It should be more functional and look nicer than it did before you started. If you have done that, you have succeeded, even if the client has a bit of trouble getting used to the new look.

Be happy in your work and keep the faith. Know that you are making an improvement worthy of your hire, even if it doesn't translate out to the more optimal, obvious and numerical results we all like to get.

Success isn't defined by how much money you make. While that's part of it, it should give you more pleasure to have done something valuable and helpful for the people who have placed their trust in you. That's what it's all about.

Thank you for going on this excursion into the realm of portfolio creation and implementation. I wish you the very best success in your business. Never give up!

A Few Final Questions and Answers About Portfolios

There are many things to consider when creating a portfolio. I decided to present some of the aspects I have not addressed so far in a question-answer format:

When is a portfolio complete?

In my eyes a portfolio is complete the minute you consider it ready to present to your audience. You can always add to your portfolio as you do more projects or start a brand new one. Obviously the more you have, the more you can circulate so that your work is working for you whether you're around or not.

Should portfolio photographs be matted or not?

No, not unless they are actual photographs on glossy paper. You should protect them in that case, but putting your materials in plastic sleeves should be sufficient.

Should all the photographs and mats be the same size?

Traditionally, if photographs are matted then the mats are all the same size. If photographs are not matted then all the sheets of paper are the same size. The image size and dimensions can and do vary, as it is not uncommon to crop images or use different camera formats in the same portfolio. However, having the mat or paper size constant does bring uniformity to the portfolio.

How many photographs should be included in a portfolio?

This depends on your particular taste and on your opinion regarding how many photographs is enough. I personally consider anything past 25 images to be way too many.

This is not to say you do not have more images worthy of being included in a portfolio. But your audience will get tired after the 25th photograph or so, if their attention lasts that long. Non-photographers rarely have what I call photographic endurance. Most viewers get tired after looking at 10 to 20 prints.

Chapter Twenty-Four

Bonuses and Additional Resources

Where to Get Rental Furniture

Go to a local furniture store or even a second hand store instead of going to a rental company (which you can also do as well, if necessary), or even a consignment store. You just may find you'll get a better deal since most furniture rental companies make you rent for 3 months minimum when you might only need 1 month. Just be careful that you don't wind up paying more for the 1 month option.

You'll want to speak to the manager or if possible the owner and try to work out a deal for advertising their store in the home you are staging for either a discount on buying their furniture or some kind of rental deal that is below the deals they offer to the general public.

You could set up an area by the front door with the store's business cards and brochures and a sign saying "Furnishings by ABC Furniture Store" or something of that nature.

You can make similar arrangements with other stores that supply accessories. This could eliminate having to purchase and stock accessories yourself.

My suggestion is that you make an appointment with the owner of the company, and only the owner. Owners will be more accommodating than employees because they will more likely be able to capture the vision of increased profits by cooperating with you. So go in and tell the owner about your business and share a little about your business plan, so that he/she can see that you are a professional looking for a long term relationship. Try to enlist the owner as a "team player". Ask the owner for suggestions on how the two of you can work together for the good of the clients you develop, so that everyone wins.

By making the owner a "member of your team", so to speak, you should not only find them more accommodating to you in the future, but then they can make plans to, perhaps, carry more items on hand that are particularly useful to you. No one is going to want to turn away business, especially if they view you as someone who will possibly increase their business by providing an expanded on-going customer base.

In that initial meeting, you can make statements such as, "Well, if I won't be able to count on you to have enough inventory on hand to meet the needs of my growing clientele, then I'll continue searching until I find the best deal, which I'd rather not do. So I'm hoping we can work together to our mutual benefit."

As for renting storage space and purchasing furniture your self to serve as props, that is always an option, but not recommended until such time as your business flow is steady and growing. When you're new, you don't want to over commit yourself.

Furniture Rental Companies

Brook Furniture Rental and Cort Furniture Rental are known to be pretty good companies for stagers. Brook is professional and they work with stagers to help your business and offer a 1 and 2 month rental. Cort is less expensive but only offers 3 month rentals as of this writing.

A local, small furniture store in town might be more open to working out a special arrangement with you. One of my students found such a local store and introduced herself to the owner who personally works the store 7 days a week. He has been the backbone to her business in the last year! He lets her rent anything in the store, allows her to browse through catalogs and in return, she has introduced 3-4 other stagers to him as well.

He has special arrangements just for these stagers, as well as discounted delivery and rental rates, month to month contracts, discounts for their clients, and so forth. She took a chance by walking in and introducing herself and thought it couldn't hurt to ask how they could help each other.

He buys and sells used furniture as well, so her intention was to find a smaller dealer that's been established for a long time to approach. As an added bonus, she recently worked for a client that wanted to get rid of a lot of furniture quickly. She called the furniture store owner on the spot and they set up an appointment for the following day for him to purchase the client's furniture. It's been a thriving partnership. So this approach is worth a shot.

She also recently started talking to him about clearing an area in his warehouse for rental staging furniture only (with pieces the group of stagers would choose out of catalogs that he would stock for them). They told him if he does that, they'll take care of a cataloging system for it and one of the stagers even offered to make a computer program to keep track of inventory and availability/

Be very specific in the details of the arrangements you work out, no matter what type of company it is. Some companies will be happy to rent to you for one month, but they charge 3 times as much with a higher delivery fee, so it's actually cheaper to rent it for 3 months.

Regarding the transporting of the furniture, you might be able to do the moving yourself or let the company move it for a pre-determined fee. If you've aligned yourself with one or more good agents with a number of vacant properties, you can move the furniture into a different home once the first one sells, if your rental contract has not expired.

Other issues that might come up are whether the client or the agent will be willing to take on the rental contract. If they balk at having their credit checked, they probably don't have good credit. So then you'll have to decide whether you want to take on the responsibility and liability yourself.

Of course, this is not ideal. It's better to get the homeowner to contract with a rental company. But that is the ideal scenario which won't happen all of the time.

If you wind up signing the contract, try to get the agent or the homeowner to agree to pay any deductible for you should something happen to the furniture. And get any and all agreements in writing. Never rely on verbal agreements.

They will stand up in court, but are much harder to prove. So get it in writing.

Buying Your Own Props

It's true that if you live in a big metropolitan area you'll have more resources locally. But if you don't live in a populated area, you're not left out. But you may need to be more creative in how you acquire your furniture. So that's when you go online - not for rental furniture - but to purchase at a deep discount.

Craig's List has proven to be a good source. Here in California we also have local Pennysavers, which are weekly classified ad driven throw away papers where individuals can advertise their furniture, garage sales and estate sales. It takes a lot of time to ferret out what you want and need, but over time you can build a nice grouping of props that you can use over and over again.

There are also the online classified ads, eBay and other sources you can investigate. Even if you purchase something old and dinged up, with a little tender loving care, you can fix up many items to use in your business and acquire them for pennies on the dollar.

One gal I know purchased almost an entire home of furniture from a young guy who needed to sell it. He must have been desperate because she picked up almost everything he had for less than $150. So be on the lookout for people who appear desperate to sell. You can get incredible bargains this way.

Whenever possible, you might also think about buying wicker sofas and chairs. They are light weight and when you spend a lot of time moving furniture from place to place, the lighter the better. If necessary spray paint the wicker to a soft neutral color and you can use it anywhere. Recover or replace the cushions as needed.

Some people store their furniture in their garage; some have a barn for storage; some rent storage spaces; some make arrangements with others who have space to rent or lease.

So think about your options first and work out the deals that will work for you and cost you the least amount of money to sustain.

Maximizing Your Props

Once you have some pretty good inventory, you can use your furniture for multi purposes in addition to staging someone's home.

For instance, when you are staging a home, take a little extra time and bring in way more than you need, but first take before pictures of the room as is. Then decorate it fully as you would on a redesign appointment. Take your after pictures. Then stage the room, removing all items that are not needed. Take more after pictures.

Now you have examples for your portfolio of how you would redesign a room and how you would stage a room. By adding a few of these to your portfolio, you'll easily be able to show the difference between a staged room and a redesigned room.

When you're talking to a home owner for staging, you'll be setting them up early on for a redesign appointment later when they have moved into their next home, assuming they move locally.

When purchasing props, it's important to do so in coordinating colors so that you can mix and match anything together for any circumstance. For this reason you might want to build an all white collection, an off white collection, a black collection and a brown collection. Stay neutral with the core basics.

You can always add some colorful accessories for drama and interest, but keep the large items (sofa, chairs, tables and so forth) as neutral as possible. This way, if needed, you could combine collections by mixing black and white together or mixing brown and off-white together.

White and black collections would be used in cool rooms; brown and off-white collections would be used in warm rooms.

If you already have or acquire non-neutral large pieces, you could consider covering them with slip covers in neutral colors. Remember, the idea in staging is not to "decorate" as you would in most other situations, but to neutralize and de-personalize the space so that potential buyers focus on the assets of the house, and not the furniture and accessories.

Your props are there to help buyers fall in love with the house; they are not there to help buyers fall in love with the furnishings.

Common Props to Acquire

Some of the more common props you might consider acquiring are (light weight items are most preferable):

Love seats	Throw pillows
Chairs	Bed pillows
Coffee table	Blankets
End tables	Throws
Area rugs	Reading glasses
Trees	Plates
Tall floor plants	Napkins
Table plants	Stainless ware
Candelabra	Glasses
Candles	Goblets
Old hardbound books	Towels
Magazines	Comforter
Trays	Slip covers
Vases	Table cloths

While this is not an exhaustive list, it is sufficient enough to get your business off the ground and produce some significant income. As your business grows, you can add to your inventory out of your profits.

Additional Marketing Tools of Value

You don't have to re-invent the wheel when it comes to creating visual aids to augment your portfolio, especially when you are new in your business and don't have the necessary evidence to support your claims. So here is a list of some visual aids, action tools and additional training you might consider to help you further and eliminate the frustrations and time needed to create your own.

Musical Slideshows on CD on Home Staging and/or Interior Redesign
Showing before and after pictures of staged homes and redesigned homes of every income bracket, along with the probable benefits usually received by such services, these slideshows help prospects see the differences staging and redesign has made for other owners. Each has a different musical background. Great for loaning to a prospect to show to their spouse.

Powerpoint Presentations with Scripts on CD on Home Staging and Interior Redesign

Series of before and after pictures of staged homes or redesigned homes from varying income brackets in a Powerpoint Presentation coupled with a fully developed and editable script. Show presentations to real estate agents or groups of homeowners interested in decorating topics.

Promotional Postcards

Variety of professionally designed and printed postcards to assist in announcing your business, pointing out the benefits of your services and the need for such services. Generic. Sold in sets of 100 per design. Several styles and messages to choose from.

Home Staging for Yourself

Thorough checklist of the most common home staging tasks suitable for most home situations. The perfect consultation guide which eliminates the need for preparing follow-up reports (80 pgs).

Can be sold as part of a consultation service or as a stand-alone product with great perceived value. Pass-through costs so these guides are free to stagers. Stagers can purchase them in small quantities of 5-10 at a time and up-charge for them to make a profit. You should always have an ample supply of these handy checklist guides with you at all times.

Additional Training of High Value

Home Staging in Tough Times

Geared to help anyone thrive and survive during tough economic times, this book delves deeper into marketing tactics that are especially good in a down market and has some of the most practical help you'll find anywhere (210 pages). Learn how to market in a cashless economy.

Home Staging for Profit

Basic Home Staging training. My masterpiece on the secrets of home stagers and how to start, develop, grow, manage and sustain a home staging business. My best selling and most popular book. This manual teaches you virtually everything from A-Z when it comes to getting a home staging business off the ground, developing it and growing it into a significant profit center. Tens of thousands of readers credit their success in the business to the material in this one manual. Available as ebook or as printed manual (256 pgs).

Staging Luxurious Homes

Secrets of developing a clientele among the affluent homeowners in any geographical area. Teaches different psychological idiosynchrasys and requirements of wealthy prospects and clients and how to build a lucrative business in the upscale neighborhoods (232 pgs).

Rearrange It!

Basic Interior Redesign training. Secrets of re-designers on how to start, develop, grow, manage and sustain an interior redesign or one day decorating business. The original manual that revolutionized the way interior re-designers learned how to do this business. This guide demystified the whole process and made a simple business easy to understand and develop. It made a lot of people mad who were selling expensive seminars but it opened up the whole industry to everyone. Available as ebook or in printed manual (176 pgs).

Décor Secrets Revealed (ebook)

Twenty five chapters on the secrets, concepts and strategies used by professional stagers and re-designers to arrange furniture and accessories. Concepts are traditionally accepted practices of interior designers everywhere (25 chapters). Over 600 color images. Available solely as an ebook and must be read on your computer. Compatible with PC or Mac.

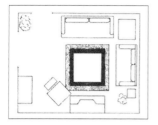

Arrange Your Stuff

The sequel to Décor Secrets Revealed, this comb-bound manual expands and emphasizes the concepts already presented in Décor Secrets Revealed (ebook). Shows multiple ways to use the same furnishings in the same room to achieve several different configurations. Great for keeping handy when on appointments to stimulate ideas (188 pgs).

Wall Groupings! Secrets of Displaying Your Art & Photos

Soft cover book that delves into the techniques professionals use to arrange wall groupings of art and photos and many other items. This is the sequel to the popular book I published in the 1980s that was used as a college textbook. It has now been upgraded and improved. Filled with photos of actual wall groupings designed by many professionals across the country. Picture hanging tips also included.

Advanced Redesign

Once your business is off the ground and you've gotten your feet wet, you might want to discover additional great techniques and tactics for getting the most profits from your business you can. This manual (or ebook) teaches you how to take your business to the next level for even more profit, leaving no stone unturned when it comes to maximizing your talent, knowledge and expertise. (200 pgs).

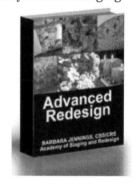

Do's and Don'ts in Home Staging and Redesign

They say we learn best from our mistakes, but that's a painful way to learn. Why not learn from the mistakes or missteps of others? This manual is filled with 101 actual staged rooms or redesigned rooms, showing the before and after pictures, plus commentary and critiques. See what works and what doesn't work and learn why and how the result could have been improved. This is a very practical, one of a kind book you won't find offered by any other trainer in the industry (240 pgs).

Upgrade to One of Our Courses

Many students get introduced to our individual products and training not knowing that we offer comprehensive certification courses as well. We have several to choose from based on your goals, your background and experience level. Please visit our website for detailed information. If you'd like to upgrade to a course that includes this manual or another one you already own, let us know before you make your selection and we'll be happy to substitute another product(s) so you don't get a duplication of products. Choose your course and in the shopping cart, on the page that asks for your shipping address, there is a notation box where you can tell us what you already own and where you bought it. We will choose a comparable substitution we feel will best help you in your journey.

Contact Information

I hope you have learned not only how to create your own powerful portfolio, but how to use it to your advantage out in the marketplace to increase your base of contacts and drive business to your doorstep. Your kind words of encouragement and referrals are always welcome with gratitude. I'm never too busy to take care of the needs of any person you refer.

For current list of products and services available, please visit our handy checklist page at:
http://www.decorate-redecorate.com/home-staging-redesign.html.

Join my brand new Face Book community by clicking "Like" at:
http://www.facebook.com/HomeStagingRedesign

Best wishes for a rewarding and prosperous journey.

Barbara Jennings, CSS/CRS
Author/Consultant

Chapter Twenty-Five

Useful Forms

On the following pages you'll see some forms I've designed for you to use when working on a project. They are needed only when doing or estimating a home staging project as they will assist you in properly estimating the amount of work and time needed to stage a home. You don't want to under estimate and not get paid what the project is worth. On the other hand, you don't want to over estimate, have the client feel you are too expensive, and lose the project altogether. So being able to arrive at a fair price is critical to your success.

These forms are free for you to use in your business but not for sharing with others. Please honor my copyright to these forms by *not* sharing them with people who have not purchased this book. To share them with others will be viewed as a copyright infringement, however, you can copy them for your own business use with my permission.

Project Estimate Worksheet

REPAIRS NEEDED

☐ Front Yard
☐ Driveway
☐ Front Door/Porch

☐ Entry
☐ Living Room
☐ Family Room
☐ Kitchen
☐ Formal Dining Room
☐ Informal Dining Room
☐ Guest Bathroom
☐ Guest Closet
☐ Den/Study/Library
☐ Halls
☐ Stairs

☐ Master Bedroom
☐ Bedroom 1
☐ Bedroom 2
☐ Bedroom 3
☐ Bedroom 4
☐ Bedroom 5
☐ Master Bath
☐ Bathroom 1
☐ Bathroom 2
☐ Bathroom 3
☐ Bathroom 4
☐ Bathroom 5
☐ Hall 1
☐ Hall 2
☐ Hall 3

☐ Laundry
☐ Linen Closet
☐ Closet 1
☐ Closet 2
☐ Closet 3

☐ Back Porch/Deck
☐ Pool
☐ Back Yard
☐ Side Yard 1
☐ Side Yard 2
☐ Garage
☐ Basement
☐ Attic

☐ Other _____
☐ Other _____
☐ Other _____
☐ Other _____
☐ Other _____

TOTAL NUMBER OF AREAS
NEEDING REPAIRS:

_____

ESTIMATED TIME NEEDED
FOR REPAIRS

_____

ESTIMATED INVESTMENT
NEEDED FOR REPAIRS

_____

Project Estimate Worksheet

COLOR CORRECTION NEEDED

☐ Front Door/Porch

☐ Entry
☐ Living Room
☐ Family Room
☐ Kitchen
☐ Formal Dining Room
☐ Informal Dining Room
☐ Guest Bathroom
☐ Guest Closet
☐ Den/Study/Library
☐ Halls
☐ Stairs

☐ Master Bedroom
☐ Bedroom 1
☐ Bedroom 2
☐ Bedroom 3
☐ Bedroom 4
☐ Bedroom 5
☐ Master Bath
☐ Bathroom 1
☐ Bathroom 2
☐ Bathroom 3
☐ Bathroom 4
☐ Bathroom 5
☐ Hall 1
☐ Hall 2
☐ Hall 3

☐ Laundry
☐ Linen Closet
☐ Closet 1
☐ Closet 2
☐ Closet 3

☐ Back Porch/Deck
☐ Garage
☐ Basement
☐ Attic

☐ Other _____
☐ Other _____
☐ Other _____
☐ Other _____
☐ Other _____

TOTAL NUMBER OF AREAS
NEEDING COLOR CHANGES:

_____

ESTIMATED TIME NEEDED
FOR COLOR CHANGES

_____

ESTIMATED INVESTMENT
NEEDED FOR COLOR
CHANGES

_____

Project Estimate Worksheet

FURNITURE REARRANGEMENT NEEDED

☐ Porch

☐ Entry
☐ Living Room
☐ Family Room
☐ Kitchen
☐ Formal Dining Room
☐ Informal Dining Room
☐ Den/Study/Library

☐ Master Bedroom
☐ Bedroom 1
☐ Bedroom 2
☐ Bedroom 3
☐ Bedroom 4
☐ Bedroom 5
☐ Master Bath

☐ Back Porch/Deck
☐ Pool
☐ Back Yard
☐ Side Yard 1
☐ Side Yard 2
☐ Basement
☐ Attic

☐ Other _____

☐ Other _____
☐ Other _____
☐ Other _____
☐ Other _____

TOTAL NUMBER OF AREAS
NEEDING
REARRANGEMENT:

_____

ESTIMATED TIME NEEDED
FOR REARRANGEMENT

_____

ESTIMATED INVESTMENT
NEEDED FOR
REARRANGEMENT

_____

Project Estimate Worksheet

CLEAN UP NEEDED

☐ Front Yard
☐ Driveway
☐ Porch

☐ Entry
☐ Living Room
☐ Family Room
☐ Kitchen
☐ Formal Dining Room
☐ Informal Dining Room
☐ Guest Bathroom
☐ Guest Closet
☐ Den/Study/Library
☐ Halls
☐ Stairs

☐ Master Bedroom
☐ Bedroom 1
☐ Bedroom 2
☐ Bedroom 3
☐ Bedroom 4
☐ Bedroom 5
☐ Master Bath
☐ Bathroom 1
☐ Bathroom 2
☐ Bathroom 3
☐ Bathroom 4
☐ Bathroom 5
☐ Hall 1
☐ Hall 2
☐ Hall 3

☐ Laundry
☐ Linen Closet
☐ Closet 1
☐ Closet 2
☐ Closet 3

☐ Back Porch/Deck
☐ Pool
☐ Back Yard
☐ Side Yard 1
☐ Side Yard 2
☐ Garage
☐ Basement
☐ Attic

☐ Other _____
☐ Other _____
☐ Other _____
☐ Other _____
☐ Other _____

TOTAL NUMBER OF AREAS
NEEDING CLEAN UP:

_____

ESTIMATED TIME NEEDED
FOR CLEAN UP

_____

ESTIMATED INVESTMENT
NEEDED FOR CLEAN UP

_____

Project Estimate Worksheet

DE-CLUTTERING NEEDED

□ Front Yard
□ /Porch

□ Entry
□ Living Room
□ Family Room
□ Kitchen
□ Formal Dining Room
□ Informal Dining Room
□ Guest Bathroom
□ Guest Closet
□ Den/Study/Library
□ Halls
□ Stairs

□ Master Bedroom
□ Bedroom 1
□ Bedroom 2
□ Bedroom 3
□ Bedroom 4
□ Bedroom 5
□ Master Bath
□ Bathroom 1
□ Bathroom 2
□ Bathroom 3
□ Bathroom 4
□ Bathroom 5
□ Hall 1
□ Hall 2
□ Hall 3

□ Laundry
□ Linen Closet
□ Closet 1
□ Closet 2
□ Closet 3

□ Back Porch/Deck
□ Pool
□ Back Yard
□ Side Yard 1
□ Side Yard 2
□ Garage
□ Basement
□ Attic

□ Other _____
□ Other _____
□ Other _____
□ Other _____
□ Other _____

TOTAL NUMBER OF AREAS
NEEDING DE-CLUTTERING:

_____

ESTIMATED TIME NEEDED
FOR DE-CLUTTERING

_____

ESTIMATED INVESTMENT
NEEDED FOR DE-
CLUTTERING

_____

Project Estimate Worksheet

ENHANCEMENT NEEDED

□ Front Yard
□ Driveway
□ Front Door/Porch

□ Entry
□ Living Room
□ Family Room
□ Kitchen
□ Formal Dining Room
□ Informal Dining Room
□ Guest Bathroom
□ Guest Closet
□ Den/Study/Library
□ Halls
□ Stairs

□ Master Bedroom
□ Bedroom 1
□ Bedroom 2
□ Bedroom 3
□ Bedroom 4
□ Bedroom 5
□ Master Bath
□ Bathroom 1
□ Bathroom 2
□ Bathroom 3
□ Bathroom 4
□ Bathroom 5
□ Hall 1
□ Hall 2
□ Hall 3

□ Laundry
□ Linen Closet
□ Closet 1
□ Closet 2
□ Closet 3

□ Back Porch/Deck
□ Pool
□ Back Yard
□ Side Yard 1
□ Side Yard 2
□ Garage
□ Basement
□ Attic

□ Other _____
□ Other _____
□ Other _____
□ Other _____
□ Other _____

TOTAL NUMBER OF AREAS
NEEDING ENHANCEMENT:

_____

ESTIMATED TIME NEEDED
FOR ENHANCEMENT

_____

ESTIMATED INVESTMENT
NEEDED FOR
ENHANCEMENT

_____

Project Estimate Worksheet

PACKING NEEDED

☐ Porch

☐ Entry
☐ Living Room
☐ Family Room
☐ Kitchen
☐ Formal Dining Room
☐ Informal Dining Room
☐ Guest Bathroom
☐ Guest Closet
☐ Den/Study/Library
☐ Halls

☐ Master Bedroom
☐ Bedroom 1
☐ Bedroom 2
☐ Bedroom 3
☐ Bedroom 4
☐ Bedroom 5
☐ Master Bath
☐ Bathroom 1
☐ Bathroom 2
☐ Bathroom 3
☐ Bathroom 4
☐ Bathroom 5
☐ Hall 1
☐ Hall 2
☐ Hall 3

☐ Laundry
☐ Linen Closet
☐ Closet 1
☐ Closet 2
☐ Closet 3

☐ Back Porch/Deck
☐ Pool
☐ Back Yard
☐ Side Yard 1
☐ Side Yard 2
☐ Garage
☐ Basement
☐ Attic

☐ Other _____
☐ Other _____
☐ Other _____
☐ Other _____
☐ Other _____

TOTAL NUMBER OF AREAS
NEEDING PACKING:

_____

ESTIMATED TIME NEEDED
FOR PACKING

_____

ESTIMATED INVESTMENT
NEEDED FOR PACKING

_____

253

Project Estimate Worksheet

REMOVAL NEEDED

□ Front Yard
□ Driveway
□ Porch

□ Entry
□ Living Room
□ Family Room
□ Kitchen
□ Formal Dining Room
□ Informal Dining Room
□ Guest Bathroom
□ Guest Closet
□ Den/Study/Library
□ Halls
□ Stairs

□ Master Bedroom
□ Bedroom 1
□ Bedroom 2
□ Bedroom 3
□ Bedroom 4
□ Bedroom 5
□ Master Bath
□ Bathroom 1
□ Bathroom 2
□ Bathroom 3
□ Bathroom 4
□ Bathroom 5
□ Hall 1
□ Hall 2
□ Hall 3

□ Laundry
□ Linen Closet
□ Closet 1
□ Closet 2
□ Closet 3

□ Back Porch/Deck
□ Pool
□ Back Yard
□ Side Yard 1
□ Side Yard 2
□ Garage
□ Basement
□ Attic

□ Other _____
□ Other _____
□ Other _____
□ Other _____
□ Other _____

TOTAL NUMBER OF AREAS
NEEDING REMOVAL:

_____

ESTIMATED TIME NEEDED
FOR REMOVAL

_____

ESTIMATED INVESTMENT
NEEDED FOR REMOVAL

_____

Project Estimate Worksheet

RENTAL FURNISHINGS NEEDED

☐ Porch

☐ Entry
☐ Living Room
☐ Family Room
☐ Kitchen
☐ Formal Dining Room
☐ Informal Dining Room
☐ Guest Bathroom
☐ Den/Study/Library

☐ Master Bedroom
☐ Bedroom 1
☐ Bedroom 2
☐ Bedroom 3
☐ Bedroom 4
☐ Bedroom 5
☐ Master Bath
☐ Bathroom 1
☐ Bathroom 2
☐ Bathroom 3
☐ Bathroom 4
☐ Bathroom 5

☐ Back Porch/Deck
☐ Back Yard
☐ Basement
☐ Attic

☐ Other _____
☐ Other _____
☐ Other _____
☐ Other _____
☐ Other _____

TOTAL NUMBER OF AREAS
NEEDING RENTALS:

_____

ESTIMATED TIME NEEDED
FOR RENTALS

_____

ESTIMATED INVESTMENT
NEEDED FOR RENTALS

_____

Project Estimate Worksheet

SUB-CONTRATORS NEEDED

□ Front Yard
□ Driveway
□ Front Door/Porch

□ Entry
□ Living Room
□ Family Room
□ Kitchen
□ Formal Dining Room
□ Informal Dining Room
□ Guest Bathroom
□ Guest Closet
□ Den/Study/Library
□ Halls
□ Stairs

□ Master Bedroom
□ Bedroom 1
□ Bedroom 2
□ Bedroom 3
□ Bedroom 4
□ Bedroom 5
□ Master Bath
□ Bathroom 1
□ Bathroom 2
□ Bathroom 3
□ Bathroom 4
□ Bathroom 5
□ Hall 1
□ Hall 2
□ Hall 3

□ Laundry
□ Linen Closet
□ Closet 1
□ Closet 2
□ Closet 3

□ Back Porch/Deck
□ Pool
□ Back Yard
□ Side Yard 1
□ Side Yard 2
□ Garage
□ Basement
□ Attic

□ Other _____
□ Other _____
□ Other _____
□ Other _____
□ Other _____

TOTAL NUMBER OF AREAS
NEEDING CONTRACTORS:

_____

ESTIMATED TIME NEEDED
FOR CONTRACTORS

_____

ESTIMATED INVESTMENT
NEEDED FOR CONTRACTORS

_____

Project Estimate Worksheet

BOXES/BAGS NEEDED

☐ Front Yard
☐ Driveway
☐ Porch

☐ Entry
☐ Living Room
☐ Family Room
☐ Kitchen
☐ Formal Dining Room
☐ Informal Dining Room
☐ Guest Bathroom
☐ Guest Closet
☐ Den/Study/Library
☐ Halls

☐ Master Bedroom
☐ Bedroom 1
☐ Bedroom 2
☐ Bedroom 3
☐ Bedroom 4
☐ Bedroom 5
☐ Master Bath
☐ Bathroom 1
☐ Bathroom 2
☐ Bathroom 3
☐ Bathroom 4
☐ Bathroom 5
☐ Hall 1
☐ Hall 2
☐ Hall 3

☐ Laundry
☐ Linen Closet
☐ Closet 1
☐ Closet 2
☐ Closet 3

☐ Back Porch/Deck
☐ Pool
☐ Back Yard
☐ Side Yard 1
☐ Side Yard 2
☐ Garage
☐ Basement
☐ Attic

☐ Other _____
☐ Other _____
☐ Other _____
☐ Other _____
☐ Other _____

TOTAL NUMBER OF AREAS
NEEDING BOXES/BAGS:

_____

ESTIMATED TIME NEEDED
FOR BOXES/BAGS

_____

ESTIMATED INVESTMENT
NEEDED FOR BOXES/BAGS

_____

Project Estimate Worksheet

PLANTS/TREES NEEDED

☐ Front Yard
☐ Drive
☐ Porch

☐ Entry
☐ Living Room
☐ Family Room
☐ Kitchen
☐ Formal Dining Room
☐ Informal Dining Room
☐ Guest Bathroom
☐ Den/Study/Library
☐ Halls
☐ Stairs

☐ Master Bedroom
☐ Bedroom 1
☐ Bedroom 2
☐ Bedroom 3
☐ Bedroom 4
☐ Bedroom 5
☐ Master Bath
☐ Bathroom 1
☐ Bathroom 2
☐ Bathroom 3
☐ Bathroom 4
☐ Bathroom 5
☐ Hall 1
☐ Hall 2
☐ Hall 3

☐ Back Porch/Deck
☐ Pool
☐ Back Yard
☐ Side Yard 1
☐ Side Yard 2
☐ Garage
☐ Basement
☐ Attic

☐ Other _____
☐ Other _____
☐ Other _____
☐ Other _____
☐ Other _____

TOTAL NUMBER OF AREAS
NEEDING PLANTS:

_____

ESTIMATED TIME NEEDED
FOR PLANTS

_____

ESTIMATED INVESTMENT
NEEDED FOR PLANTS

_____

Project Estimate Worksheet

ACCESSORIES NEEDED

□ Porch

□ Entry
□ Living Room
□ Family Room
□ Kitchen
□ Formal Dining Room
□ Informal Dining Room
□ Guest Bathroom
□ Den/Study/Library
□ Halls
□ Stairs

□ Master Bedroom
□ Bedroom 1
□ Bedroom 2
□ Bedroom 3
□ Bedroom 4
□ Bedroom 5
□ Master Bath
□ Bathroom 1
□ Bathroom 2
□ Bathroom 3
□ Bathroom 4
□ Bathroom 5
□ Hall 1
□ Hall 2
□ Hall 3

□ Laundry

□ Back Porch/Deck
□ Back Yard
□ Basement
□ Attic

□ Other _____
□ Other _____
□ Other _____
□ Other _____
□ Other _____

TOTAL NUMBER OF AREAS
NEEDING ACCESSORIES:

_____

ESTIMATED TIME NEEDED
FOR ACCESSORIES

_____

ESTIMATED INVESTMENT
NEEDED FOR ACCESSORIES

_____

Project Estimate Summary

Repairs Needed $_____

Color Correction Needed $_____

Rearrangement Needed $_____

Clean Up Needed $_____

De-Cluttering Needed $_____

Enhancement Needed $_____

Packing Needed $_____

Removal Needed $_____

Rental of Furniture (if any) $_____

Sub-Contractors Needed $_____

Boxes/Bags Needed $_____

Plants Needed $_____

Supplies Needed $_____

Accessories Needed $_____

Miscellaneous Needs $_____

Total Estimate $_____

NOTE: This is only an estimate to assist in establishing a working budget. Final figure may be more or less depending on individual circumstances and unforeseen obstacles and needs. Our goal always is to complete a project in less time and under budget.

Testimonial Request

I go out on a job interview every time I call on a new prospective homeowner or real estate agent. Who would ever go out on a job interview without a reference letter? This gives me the power to hire or fire myself every day. Please help me get hired by writing a brief letter of reference below or drawing one up within the next 24 hours for me to pick up. Just let me know your preference.

_____

_____

_____

_____

_____

_____

_____

_____

_____

_____

_____

_____

_____

_____

_____

_____

_____

_____

_____

_____

_____

_____

_____

_____

_____

_____   _____
Signature   Date

Proposed Sub-Contractor List

The following sub-contractors will be needed to provide services for client listed here:

_____

NAME   **PHONE NUMBER**

_____
_____
_____
_____
_____
_____
_____
_____
_____
_____
_____
_____
_____
_____
_____
_____
_____
_____
_____
_____
_____
_____
_____

Unsolicited Testimonials

"I would also like to take the time to tell you that I have learned a great deal from your materials, and the certification process has given both of us a chance to apply the lessons we have learned. We have grown with each project and feel much more prepared to go out there and really get our business going. Roomworks - Staging & Redesign, LLC: Jeanette Lair Nancy Hinsch"

"I recently purchased Home Staging for Profit, Rearrange It, and Advanced Redesign, which I am enjoying very much! . . . Also, wanted to let you know that last year I took an interior decorating class from an online college and received a diploma from them, but I must admit your books are much more informative. Thank you, Gayle Mitchell"

"Hi Barbara, Thank you for this delightful course. I am enjoying all the materials. I have been studying staging for about 8 months and reading as many books as I could get my hands on! Even though I have a Home Economics degree and have worked in the home improvement industry for 17 years, I still needed something to help me with my confidence. With my husbands encouragement I decided that what I needed was a course and a certification. I'm very glad I chose yours because I believe that my philosophy of home design is similar to yours. . . . Thanks again and I look forward to many years of contact with you. Pam Elkins, Diamond Standard"

"Thank You Barbara! Your course is by far the BEST there is! Sandy Chisholm (Diamond Course, Certified CSS/CRS)"

"Hi Barbara, I wanted to thank you for your informative business manual. I had small business training and an 'instinct' for staging, but your manual answered my specific questions about getting THIS business up and running successfully. Not only that, but your information on how to conduct a consultation in a step-by-step presentation helped me get over my nerves and make that first call." - Shannon Emmanuel

43920924R00147

Made in the USA
Lexington, KY
17 August 2015